D0945423

Sing
and
Rejoice!

New Hymns for Congregations

Orlando Schmidt
Compiler and Editor

HERALD PRESS
Scottdale, Pennsylvania
Kitchener, Ontario
1979

SING AND REJOICE!
Copyright © 1979 by Herald Press, Scottdale, Pa. 15683
    Published simultaneously in Canada by Herald Press,
    Kitchener, Ont. N2G 4M5
Library of Congress Catalog Card Number: 79-84367
International Standard Book Numbers:
    0-8361-1210-5 (hardcover)
    0-8361-1211-3 (softcover)
Printed in the United States of America
Design: Tom Hershberger

15 14 13 12 11 10 9 8 7 6 5 4 3 2 1

Herald Press gratefully acknowledges the cooperation of individuals, publishers, and trusts who have granted permission to include copyrighted songs in this book. We have carefully endeavored to ascertain the copyright status of each piece. If any songs have been included without proper permission or credit, we will upon notification gladly make necessary corrections in future editions.

Introduction

Only 10 percent of the material in today's standard hymnals was produced in the twentieth century. Less than 5 percent was created during the past fifty years. *Sing and Rejoice!* is an attempt to supplement the rich heritage of the past with texts and tunes from recent decades.

The present generation has witnessed an explosion of creativity in church music. It is unparalleled in this century, and has contributed a superabundance of hymns. The significance of this hymnic surge is not only the large number of selections but also the variety of styles in which they are produced. Christian hymns have emerged in all secular and popular idioms, providing a body of song quite different from traditional music for worship.

This, of course, is not new in the history of the church. Times of renewal have normally been characterized by infusion of secular music. Luther transformed street songs into chorales. Hundreds of Wesley's hymns were sung to everyday music and secular melodies. Worldly tunes for sacred texts were particularly widespread in the first half of nineteenth-century America. Older ballads and love songs from England replaced psalm tunes of earlier years. Later in the century popular songs provided the style for hymns used in camp meetings and revivals.

Basis for Selection

Sing and Rejoice! reflects a predominance of *contemporary* materials, in various styles, but incorporating also some older selections that provide continuity with traditional worship. A majority of hymns represent new texts and new tunes (e.g., 1, 8, 37, 133, 144). Several dozen old texts have been set to new tunes (e.g., 35, 114, 117, 137). Some new texts are sung to old tunes (e.g., 12, 23, 26, 147). More than twenty numbers provide both older texts and tunes, generally not available in standard hymnals (e.g., 5, 38, 80, 140). These include a dozen Negro spirituals (e.g., 27, 46, 66, 90, 124) and several traditional texts with folk tunes.

Hymns have been chosen to be sung by the congregation. Countless hymns produced in recent years are clearly more suitable for soloists or small groups than for larger congregations. For this collection the question regarding suitability for a worshiping congregation was consistently asked. This does not imply that all the hymns will be easy. All of them, however, are within the reach of the normal congregation, given appropriate leadership, adequate accompaniment, and repeated singing.

Some discernment has been exercised regarding *lasting qualities* of hymns. A number of selections, "Let There Be Peace," "Yours Is the Kingdom," and "The Spirit of the Lord," have clearly demonstrated their worth by repeated use. Folk tunes from other countries, such as "Now the Green Blade Riseth" and "Song of Good News," as well as the spirituals, have proved useful. It is normal for some hymns to be short-lived, catching on rapidly, but becoming tiresome after a while.

Since the Christian church is a worldwide body of believers, an effort has been made to give this collection of hymns a *cosmopolitan* flavor. This has been possible through the growing availability of hymns from other countries, not least of which was *Cantate Domino,* produced for the 1975 gathering of Christians in Kenya. So we have tunes and texts from Nigeria, Tanzania, Sri Lanka, Indonesia, Hungary, Jamaica, Cheyenne Americans, and many other peoples and places.

A chief goal has been to reflect the *concerns of the church today:* discipleship, unity, fellowship, mission and outreach, obedience and covenant, social action, the reality of the Holy Spirit, love, peace, hope, freedom, joy, Christian experience, and devotion. There are hymns for love feasts and other celebrations of the Lord's Supper.

Suggestions for Singing

Unison singing is a distinguishing feature of today's hymns. It requires a dependable accompaniment played with keyboard, guitar, or a combination of various instruments. While many of the hymns in this book provide an accompaniment for keyboard, others simply indicate chords to be played. This enables instrumentalists to improvise in their own style, which should always provide a dependable rhythm. Sometimes an alternate set of chords, to lower or raise the pitch, is indicated.

Part singing is possible with many of these hymns. Often tunes are arranged precisely for four-part singing (e.g., 5, 36, 96, 131). Others have an accompaniment that makes it easy to sing in parts, even though the notes are not arranged for it (e.g., 53, 84, 95). There are at least fourteen rounds or canons (e.g., 2, 56, 115). Parts can be improvised for some unison melodies, especially when the accompaniment provides a good, harmonic foundation (e.g., 111, 143, 144).

Solo voices can be used with many hymns that have a refrain, with the soloist singing the stanzas and the congregation joining in the refrain. This is a good way to learn an unfamiliar hymn (e.g., 32, 54, 67, 70, 97, 135). After hearing a soloist sing the stanzas, a congregation will be able to sing them too. Or a small group can learn a hymn, singing it for a congregation with the intention of having the larger group sing it eventually.

Although this collection has been assembled with the congregation in mind, it will provide some materials for church choirs (e.g., 18, 85, 116, 141), for smaller choral groups, for soloists, and for young people's activities. These hymns invite the use of *imagination* when they are accepted as an expression of worship. Harmonizing melodic lines, improvising accompaniments, experimenting with a simple obbligato, forming rhythmic groups of percussion, singing antiphonally—these are some possibilities.

It has been the hope and prayer of many people that this set of hymns will enrich the worship of congregations and that it will be helpful in understanding and expressing the gospel of Jesus Christ for our time.

It is not possible to mention all the people who have contributed to this project. For initial help and continuing support I especially thank Lois Bergen, Lauren Friesen, Neil Matthies, Lora Oyer, and David Habegger, who provided the initial impetus for this collection. Helpful suggestions were also given by Mary Oyer, Erik Routley, Esther and George Wiebe, and others.

Orlando Schmidt
February, 1979

1. A Cry in the Night

Geoffrey Ainger

Ian Calvert
Accomp., O. S.

1 A cry in the night And a child is born;
2 A Friend for the poor And the ho - ly frown;
3 A trial in the dark, The dis - ci - ples run.
4 A Man on a cross, And the sun beats down.

A child in a sta - ble, There is - n't an - y room.
He joins in their par - ties, They scan - dal - ize the town.
They bring Him to Pi - late, He stands there all a - lone.
Up there on the gal - lows He's got a thorn - y crown.

A cry in the night and God has
A Friend for the poor and God has
A trial in the dark and God has
A Man on a cross and God has

made Our home - less - ness His home.
made Our home - less - ness His home.
made Our home - less - ness His home.
made Our home - less - ness His home.

5 A voice in the dawn When the women came:
   "You're looking for Jesus; Don't seek Him in a tomb."
A voice in the dawn and God has made Our homelessness His home.

Reprinted from *Songs from Notting Hill*, 1963.

2. Agape Meal Song

(A 4-part Round)

Al Carmines
Al Carmines

Food and drink and warmth and light, Smell and taste and touch and sight,

We are em-braced by life___ We are em-braced by love.

Life is wid - er than our minds, Love is wis - er

than our hearts And ev - 'ry - thing is more than I.

But I am a part. See - ing you I know my - self,

Touch-ing you I touch the Lord So I speak the word___

And I sing the song. Love, life, hope, joy; love, life, hope, joy.

3. Alleluia No. 1

Don Fishel

Don Fishel
Arr. by Betty Pulkingham

Rich and broad

Refrain

Al - le - lu - ia, al - le - lu - ia, give thanks to the ris-en Lord, Al - le - lu - ia, al - le - lu - ia, give praise to His name.

Stanzas

1 Je - sus is Lord of all the earth. He is the
2 Spread the good news o'er all the earth. Je - sus has
3 We have been cru - ci - fied with Christ. Now we shall
4 God has pro-claimed the just re - ward, Life for all
5 Come let us praise the liv - ing God, Joy - ful - ly

King of cre - a - tion. name.
died and has ris - en.
live for - ev - er. Al - le -
men, al - le - lu - ia.
sing to our Sav - ior.

4. Alabaré

Anonymous

Unknown

*A - la - ba - ré, a - la - ba - ré, a - la - ba - ré a mi Se - ñor.

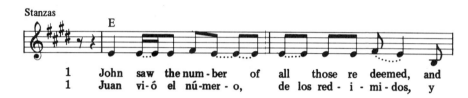

A - la - ba - ré, a - la - ba - ré, a - la - ba - ré a mi Se - ñor. ñor.

to Stanza

Stanzas

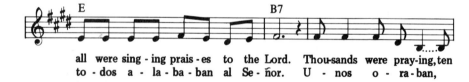

1 John saw the num - ber of all those re deemed, and
1 Juan vi - ó el nú - mer - o, de los red - i - mi - dos, y

all were sing - ing prais - es to the Lord. Thou-sands were pray-ing, ten
to - dos a - la - ba - ban al Se - ñor. U - nos o - ra-ban,

thou-sands re - joic - ing, and all were sing - ing prais - es to the Lord.
o - tros can - ta - ban, y to - dos a - la - ba - ban al Se - ñor.

to refrain

**2 There is no God as great as You, O Lord, there is none, there is
**2 No hay Dios tan gran - de co - mo Tu, No lo hay, no lo

* Alabaré a mi Señor = " I will praise my Lord."
**The second stanza is commonly sung as a separate hymn, without a refrain, in Latin - American countries.

none. There is no   none. There is no   God who does the might-y
hay.   No hay   hay.   No hay   Dios que pue-de ha - cer las

won-ders that the Lord our God has done. There is no   done. Nei-ther with an
o - bras co - mo las que ha - ces Tú.   No hay   Tú. No es con es-

ar - my, nor with their wea - pons, but by the Ho - ly Spir-it's
pa - da, ni con e - jér - ci - to, más con su San-to Es-pí - ri

power. Nei-ther with an power. And e - ven moun - tains shall be
tu. No es con es- tu. Y e - sos mon - tes se mo - ve-

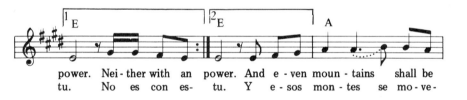

moved. And e - ven moun - tains shall be moved. And e - ven
rán. Y e - sos mon - tes se mo - ve - rán. Y e - sos

to refrain

moun - tains shall be moved. By the Ho - ly Spir - it's power.
mon - tes se mo - ve - rán. Con su San-to Es - pí - ri - tu.

5. And Can It Be

Charles Wesley

SAGINA
Thomas Campbell

1 And can it be that I should gain An in - t'rest in the
2 'Tis mys-t'ry all! Th' im-mor - tal dies! Who can ex - plore His
3 He left His Fa - ther's throne a - bove. So free, so in - fin -
4 Long my im - pris - oned Spir - it lay Fast bound in sin and

Sav - ior's blood? Died He for me, who caused His pain? For me, who
strange de - sign? In vain the first-born ser - aph tries To sound the
nite His grace? Emp - tied Him-self of all but love And bled for
na - ture's night; Thine eye dif - fused a quick-ening ray. I woke, the

Him to death pur-sued? A - maz-ing love! How can it be That
depths of love di - vine! 'Tis mer - cy all! Let earth a - dore, Let
A - dam's help -less race; 'Tis mer - cy all, im - mense and free; For,
dun - geon flamed with light; My chains fell off, my heart was free; I

A - maz - ing love! How

Thou, my God, should'st die for me? A - maz-ing love!
an - gel minds in - quire no more. 'Tis mer - cy all!
O my God, it found out me. 'Tis mer - cy all,
rose, went forth, and fol - lowed Thee. My chains fell off,

can it be that Thou, my God, should'st die for me?

How can it be That Thou, my God, should'st die for me?
Let earth a - dore, Let an-gel minds in - quire no more.
im -mense and free; For, O my God, it found out me.
my heart was free; I rose, went forth, and fol-lowed Thee.

5 No condemnation now I dread;
   Jesus and all in Him, is mine!
   Alive in Him, my living Head,
   And clothed in righteousness divine,
‖: Bold I approach the eternal throne,
   And claim the crown, through Christ my own. :‖

6. Blessed Word of God

A. M. Jones, 1969   Yoruba tune

1 Bless - ed Word of God, bless - ed Word of God,
2 Ho - ly Word of God, ho - ly Word of God,
3 Sweet - est Word of God, sweet - est Word of God,
4 Word of sins for - given, Word of sins for - given,
5 Word of truth and life, Word of truth and life,
6 Joy - ous Word of God, joy - ous Word of God,

light of the fal - ter - ing steps of men, bless - ed Word of God.
draw - ing our hearts up to God a - bove, ho - ly Word of God.
mes - sage of love com-ing down from heav'n, sweet-est Word of God.
Word of sal - va - tion's re -deem-ing love, Word of sins for - given.
teach-ing of Je - sus, our way and guide, Word of truth and life.
lead - ing us all to the joys of heav'n, joy - ous Word of God.

Reproduced by permission of the publishers, Lutterworth Press, Guildford and London,
from *Africa Praise*, © A. M. Jones.

7. As Jacob with Travel Was Weary One Day

JACOB'S LADDER

Traditional English
based on Genesis 28:10-22

Melody: English folk song
Harmony: Jack Noble White (b. 1938)

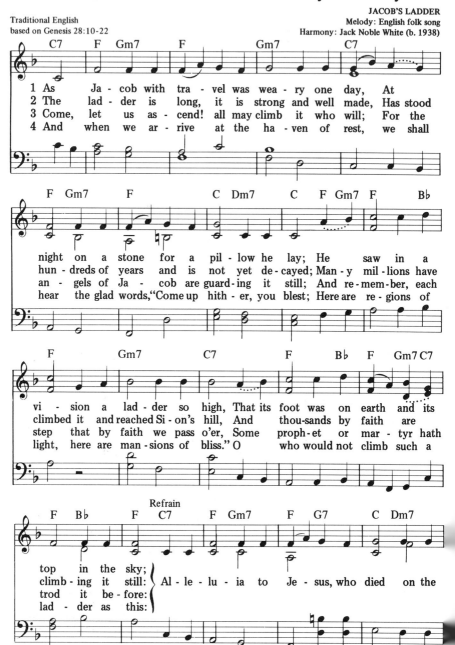

1 As Jacob with travel was weary one day, At
  night on a stone for a pillow he lay; He saw in a
  vision a ladder so high, That its foot was on earth and its
  top in the sky;

2 The ladder is long, it is strong and well made, Has stood
  hundreds of years and is not yet decayed; Many millions have
  climbed it and reached Sion's hill, And thousands by faith are
  climbing it still: { Alleluia to Jesus, who died on the

3 Come, let us ascend! all may climb it who will; For the
  angels of Jacob are guarding it still; And remember, each
  step that by faith we pass o'er, Some prophet or martyr hath
  trod it before:

4 And when we arrive at the haven of rest, we shall
  hear the glad words, "Come up hither, you blest; Here are regions of
  light, here are mansions of bliss." O who would not climb such a
  ladder as this:

Refrain

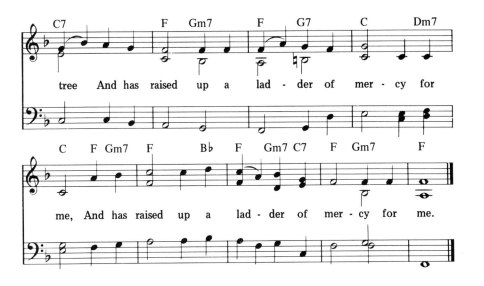

tree And has raised up a lad - der of mer - cy for

me, And has raised up a lad - der of mer - cy for me.

8. Bird of Heaven

Sydney Carter

Sydney Carter

1 Catch the Bird of heav - en, Lock Him in a cage of gold;
2 Lock Him in re - li - gion, Gold and frank - in - cense and myrrh,
3 Tem - ple made of mar - ble, Beak and feath - er made of gold,
4 Bell and book and can - dle, Can - not hold Him an - y - more,

Look a - gain to - mor - row And He will be gone.
Car - ry to His pri - son, But He will be gone.
All the bells are ring - ing, But the Bird has gone.
For the bird is fly - ing As He did be - fore.

Ah! the Bird of heav - en! Fol - low where the Bird has gone;

Ah! the Bird of heav - en! Keep on trav - el - ing on.

9. An Israeli Blessing

Original German text: Helmut Koenig

Helmut Koenig
Based on an Israeli tune

To be sung antiphonally by groups 1 and 2

1 Go   in peace, and God be   with you; 2 Sleep in peace, God hold you fast!
1 Ge - he ein   in dei-nen Frie-den! 2 Schla-fe dei - nen gu-ten Schlaf!

1 Take your ease from dai - ly   du - ty; 2 af - ter la - bor rest at   last!
1 Ruh   dich aus nach dei-ner   Ar - beit, 2 und ge - seg - net sei die Nacht!

1 Moon-light shares a   glimpse of hea-ven's mirth, 2 dew - fall fresh - ens
1 Mond-licht fliesst her - ab vom Him-mels-zelt, 2 und   der Tau glänzt

flow - ers of earth. 1 Thank God for day and night. 2 Thank God
auf un - serm Feld. 1 Preist den   Tag und die Nacht! 2 Preist die

1 & 2 together

for   dark and light. For   the sun and   for all things liv - ing
Nacht und den Tag! Preist die Son - ne, prei - set die Er - de,

to   their Lord prais - es giv - ing! A - men! A - men!
preist den Hern al - ler Wel - ten.

10. As the Deer for Water Longs
(Como el Ciervo)

Psalm 42
Original text, Spanish
Tr. by Sara Claassen

A. Mejia

1 As the deer for wa-ter longs, So we yearn for You, O God.
2 Those who hear me when I cry Say to me, "Now where is God?"
3 Soon my weep-ing will be done, For my Sa-vior is the Lord.
4 Glo-ry to the Fa-ther, Glo-ry to His on-ly Son.

Thirst-ing for the spring of life, Foun-tain of e-ter-nal love.
But the Lord is in my heart As we cel-e-brate in song.
In the pain of suf-fer-ing I will think of You, O Lord.
Glo-ry to the Spir-it, Who u-nites us in His love.

Refrain

Walk-ing, on-ward as we go, with our joy-ful songs of praise,

To Your al-tar now we come Just to love You more, O Lord.

1 Como el ciervo al agua va,
   vamos hacia Ti, Señor,
   pues de Ti tenemos sed,
      fuente del eterno amor.

2 Quien escucha mi gemir
   dice:¿dónde está tu Dios?
   El Señor se encuentra aquí
      en la voz de júbilo.

3 Ya mi llanto ha de cesar;
   El Señor es Salvador.
   Cuando tenga que sufrir
      en Ti pensaré, Señor.

4 Gloria al Padre eterno,
   gloria al Hijo Redentor,
   gloria al Espíritu
      que nos une en el amor.

Coro: Caminamos hacia Ti
         con alegres cánticos;
      hoy venimos a tu altar,
         para amarte más, Señor.

11. Born Is He, Little Child

Tr. from the French by John Morrison

18th - Century French

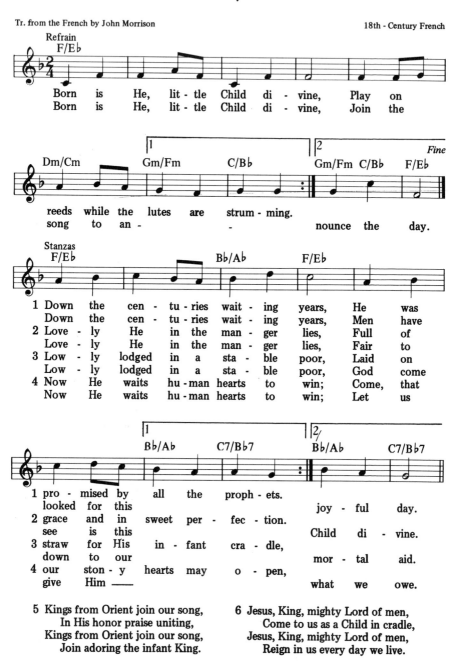

Refrain

Born is He, lit-tle Child di-vine, Play on
Born is He, lit-tle Child di-vine, Join the

reeds while the lutes are strum-ming.
song to an- - nounce the day.

Stanzas

1 Down the cen-tu-ries wait-ing years, He was
  Down the cen-tu-ries wait-ing years, Men have
2 Love-ly He in the man-ger lies, Full of
  Love-ly He in the man-ger lies, Fair to
3 Low-ly lodged in a sta-ble poor, Laid on
  Low-ly lodged in a sta-ble poor, God come
4 Now He waits hu-man hearts to win; Come, that
  Now He waits hu-man hearts to win; Let us

1 pro-mised by all the proph-ets.
  looked for this joy-ful day.
2 grace and in sweet per-fec-tion.
  see is this Child di-vine.
3 straw for His in-fant cra-dle,
  down to our mor-tal aid.
4 our ston-y hearts may o-pen,
  give Him —— what we owe.

5 Kings from Orient join our song,
   In His honor praise uniting,
  Kings from Orient join our song,
   Join adoring the infant King.

6 Jesus, King, mighty Lord of men,
   Come to us as a Child in cradle,
  Jesus, King, mighty Lord of men,
   Reign in us every day we live.

12. Christ Is Alive! Let Christians Sing

Brian Wren, written in 1968,
in memory of Dr. Martin Luther King, Jr.

TRURO
T. Williams' *Psalmodia Evangelica*, 1789

1 Christ is a - live! Let Chris - tians sing. His cross stands
2 Christ is a - live! No long - er bound To dis - tant
3 Not throned a - bove, re - mote - ly high, Un - touched, un -
4 In ev - 'ry in - sult, rift, and war, Where col - or
5 Christ is a - live! As - cend - ant Lord, He rules the

emp - ty to the sky. Let streets and homes with
years in Pal - es - tine, He comes to claim the
moved by hu - man pains, But dai - ly, in the
scorn, or wealth di - vide, He suf - fers still, yet
world His Fa - ther made, Till in the end, His

prais - es ring. His love in death shall nev - er die.
here and now. And con - quer ev - 'ry place and time.
midst of life, Our Sav - ior with the Fa - ther reigns.
loves the more, And lives, though ev - er cru - ci - fied.
love a - dored Shall be to ev - 'ry man dis - played.

Words used by permission from *Sing!* published by Fortress Press, Philadelphia, 1969.

13. By the Babylonian Rivers

Text by E. J. Bash
Based on Psalm 137: 1-4

Latvian melody
Arr. by John Ylvisaker, 1964

1 By the Bab - y - lon-ian riv - ers We sat down in grief and wept;
2 There our cap - tors in de - ri - sion Did re - quire of us a song;
3 How shall we sing the Lord's song In a strange and bit - ter land;
4 Let Thy cross be ben - e - dic - tion For men bound in ty - ran - ny;

Hanged our harps up - on a wil - low, Mourned for Zi - on when we slept.
So we sat with star - ing vi - sion, And the days were hard and long.
Can our voi - ces veil the sor - row? Lord God, hold Thy ho - ly band.
By the pow'r of res - ur - rec - tion Loose them from cap - ti - vi - ty.

Note: This hymn is a prayer for modern refugees or victims of tyranny.

Reprinted by permission from *Songs for Today*, published by the Youth Department, Minneapolis, 1964. American Lutheran Church,

14. Come, Holy Ghost

Veni Creator Spiritus
Rabanus Maurus (776-856?)
Tr. Edward Caswall, 1849, alt.

Traditional
Louis Lambillotte, S.J.

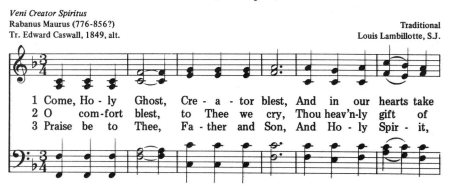

1 Come, Ho - ly Ghost, Cre - a - tor blest, And in our hearts take
2 O com-fort blest, to Thee we cry, Thou heav'n-ly gift of
3 Praise be to Thee, Fa - ther and Son, And Ho - ly Spir - it,

up Thy rest; Come with Thy grace and heav'n-ly aid To fill the
God most high; Thou font of life, and fire of love, And sweet a-
three in one; And may the Son on us be-stow The gifts that

hearts which Thou hast made, To fill the hearts which Thou hast made.
noint- ing from a - bove, And sweet a - noint- ing from a - bove.
from the Spir - it flow, The gifts that from the Spir - it flow.

15. Come, My Way, My Truth, My Life

Ralph Vaughan Williams (1872-1958)
Harmony, O. S.

George Herbert (1593-1632)

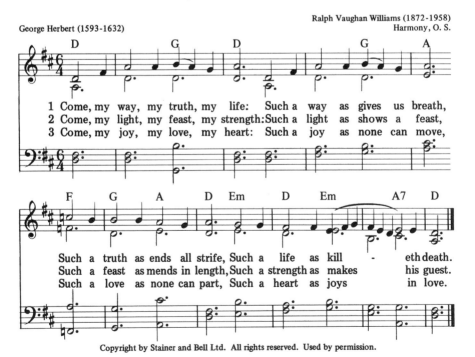

D   G   D   G   A

1 Come, my way, my truth, my life: Such a way as gives us breath,
2 Come, my light, my feast, my strength: Such a light as shows a feast,
3 Come, my joy, my love, my heart: Such a joy as none can move,

F   G   A   D   Em   D   Em   A7   D

Such a truth as ends all strife, Such a life as kill - eth death.
Such a feast as mends in length, Such a strength as makes his guest.
Such a love as none can part, Such a heart as joys in love.

16. Christ Is Changing Everything

Norman C. Habel

Richard Koehneke

1 I know we spin on earth be - neath a danc-ing sky,
2 I hear the tu - lips laugh be - neath the win - ter snow,
3 I sense an un - seen world be - yond the swirl-ing sun,
4 I know some give their eyes to those who lose their sight,

I hear a word from God that frees us all to fly.
I've seen how lit - tle child - ren make their par - ents grow,
I look for mys - ter - ies that have - n't yet be - gun,
I've seen them take His ho - ly meal and dance all night,

I feel the bones of mar - tyred ones will soon a - rise,
I'm sure that mir - a - cles can set the heav'ns a - glow,
I trust in hands of love to heal the wrongs we've done,
I want to cel - e - brate my death with all my might,

For I be - lieve that Christ is chang - ing ev - 'ry - thing,

ev - 'ry-thing, ev - 'ry - thing, ev - 'ry-thing, ev - 'ry - thing.

Tune and words (adapted by permission) from *For Mature Adults Only*, by Norman C. Habel,
copyright 1969 by Fortress Press, Philadelphia.

17. Come and See

(Children's Song)

Marilyn Houser Hamm · Marilyn Houser Hamm

1 "Come and see, come and see, I am the way and the truth," said He.

"Fol - low Me, Fol - low Me, Come as a child, O come and see."

Chris - te, Chris - te, A - do - ra - mus te,

2 Ky - ri - e, Ky - ri - e, Ky - ri - e e - le - i - son,

Al - le - lu - ia, Ky - ri - e e - le - i - son.

Chris - te, Chris - te, Chris - te, e - le - i - son.

18. Down to Earth as a Dove

PERSONENT HODIE
From *Piae Cantiones*, 1582
Arr. by Gustav T. Holst (1874-1934)

Fred Kaan (b. 1929)

1 Down to earth as a dove came to man ho-ly love; Je-sus Christ from a-bove bring-ing great sal-va-tion,

2 This is love come to light, now is fear put to flight; dark-est night giv-ing all our sor-rows

3 Christ the Lord comes to feed hung-ry men in their need; In the house there is bread; Je-sus in a sta-ble:

19. Every Star Shall Sing a Carol

Sydney Carter

EVERY STAR
Sydney Carter (b. 1915)

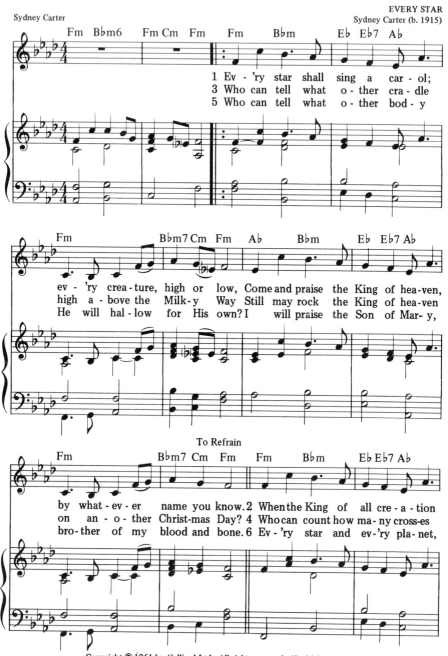

1 Ev - 'ry star shall sing a car - ol;
3 Who can tell what o - ther cra - dle
5 Who can tell what o - ther bod - y

ev - 'ry crea - ture, high or low, Come and praise the King of hea - ven,
high a - bove the Milk - y Way Still may rock the King of hea - ven,
He will hal - low for His own? I will praise the Son of Mar - y,

To Refrain

by what - ev - er name you know. 2 When the King of all cre - a - tion
on an - o - ther Christ - mas Day? 4 Who can count how ma - ny cross - es
bro - ther of my blood and bone. 6 Ev - 'ry star and ev - 'ry pla - net,

20. Fear Not! Rejoice and Be Glad

Adapted from the Book of Joel

Priscilla Wright Porter

With breadth

Refrain

Fear not, re - joice and be glad, the
Lord hath done a great thing: hath poured out His Spir - it on
all man - kind, on those who con - fess His name. *Fine*

Stanzas

1 The fig tree is bud - ding, the vine bear - eth fruit, the
2 Ye shall eat in plen - ty and be sat - is - fied, the
3 My peo - ple shall know ___ that I am the Lord, their
4 My chil - dren shall dwell in a bod - y of love, a

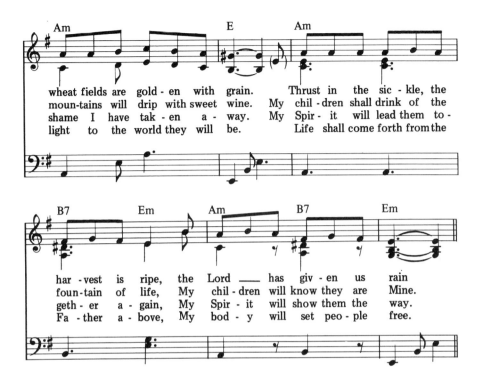

wheat fields are gold-en with grain. Thrust in the sic-kle, the
moun-tains will drip with sweet wine. My chil-dren shall drink of the
shame I have tak-en a - way. My Spir - it will lead them to -
light to the world they will be. Life shall come forth from the

har - vest is ripe, the Lord ___ has giv - en us rain
foun-tain of life, My chil-dren will know they are Mine.
geth - er a - gain, My Spir - it will show them the way.
Fa - ther a - bove, My bod - y will set peo - ple free.

21. God Is So Good

Unknown

African Christian folk song

God is so good, God is so good,

God is so good, He's so good to me.

Other stanzas may be added.

22. Fill My Cup, Lord

Richard Blanchard   Richard Blanchard

1 Like the wom-an at the well I was seek-ing For things that could not sat-is-fy; And then I heard my Sav-ior speak-ing: "Draw from My well that nev-er shall run dry."

2 There are mil-lions in this world who are crav-ing The pleas-ure earth-ly things af-ford; But none can match the won-drous treas-ure That I find in Je-sus Christ my Lord.

3 So, all peo-ple, if the things this world gave you Leave hun-gers that won't pass a-way, My bless-ed Lord will come and save you, If you kneel to Him and hum-bly pray:

Refrain

Fill my cup, Lord, I lift it up, Lord, Come and quench this thirst-ing of my soul; Bread of heav-en,

feed me till I want no more; Fill my cup, fill it up and make me whole!

23. Give Thanks to God, Who Leads Us

Iris McCoy, 1967

LAUDES DOMINI
Joseph Barnby, 1868

1 Give thanks to God, who leads us, With vast en - rich - ing love
2 The truths of our tra - di - tions Are frag-ments from the wealth
3 O God, we know our weak-ness, And pray Your glow - ing strength

In - to this u - ni - ty. Our path with Him is clear,
Of God's mag - ni - fi - cence; Each giv - ing from the store,
To weld us close in love. We seek Your Spir - it's power,

His will for us is here, That we shall be as one.
And each re - ceiv - ing more, As we grow in - to one.
In this, and ev - 'ry hour, To keep us, Lord, as one.

24. Fill My House

Peter Kearney

Peter Kearney
Arr. by Esther Wiebe

Descant for flute, recorder or violin

F/D   C7/A7

1 Fill my
2 Take my
3 Christ our
4 Join with

F/D   C/A

house un - to the full - est, Eat my
time un - to the full - est, Find in
Lord with love e - nor - mous, From the
me as one in Christ's love, May our

25. Each Morning Brings Us

Johannes Zwick
Tr. Margaret Barclay

German melody

Melody

1 Each morn - ing brings us fresh out-poured The lov - ing - kind-ness
2 The dark - ness in us, Lord, dis - pel, From bit - ter - ness, oh,
3 O God, Thou star of dawn-ing day, Give us that light for

Second voice

The lov - ing - kind -
From bit - ter - ness
Give us that light

of the Lord, It ends not as the day is past,
shield us well, From ill de - sires, from cloud - ed sight,
which we pray, Make Thou the flame in us to glow

- - ness of the Lord.
oh shield us well.
for which we pray.

But gives us strength while life shall last.
Oh do Thou lead us day and night.
That we no lack of grace may know.

But gives us strength while life shall last.
Oh do Thou lead us day and night.
That we no lack of grace may know.

26. For the Healing of the Nations

Fred Kaan (b. 1929)

REGENT SQUARE
Henry Smart, 1867

1 For the heal - ing of the na - tions, Lord, we pray with
2 Lead us, Fa - ther, in - to free - dom, from de - spair Your
3 All that kills a - bun - dant liv - ing, let it from the
4 You, Cre - a - tor - God, have writ - ten Your great name on

one ac - cord; For a just and e - qual shar - ing
world re - lease; That re - deemed from war and ha - tred,
earth be banned; Pride of sta - tus, race, or school - ing,
hu - man - kind; For our grow - ing in Your like - ness

of the things that earth af - fords. To a life of
men may come and go in peace. Show us how through
dog - mas keep - ing man from man. In our com - mon
bring the life of Christ to mind; That by our re -

love in ac - tion help us rise and pledge our word.
care and good - ness fear will die and hope in - crease.
quest for jus - tice may we hal - low life's brief span.
sponse and ser - vice earth its des - ti - ny may find.

Alternate tunes: SICILIAN MARINERS or CWM RHONDDA.

27. Give Me Jesus

Negro spiritual

Negro spiritual
Arr. by Peter D. Smith

1 Oh when I come to die,
2 In the morn - ing* when I rise,
3 Dark mid - night was my cry,
4 I heard the mourn - er say,

Oh when I come to die,
In the morn - ing when I rise,
Dark mid - night was my cry,
I heard the mourn - er say,

Oh when I come to die, give me Je - sus,
In the morn-ing when I rise, give me Je - sus,
Dark mid - night was my cry, give me Je - sus,
I heard the mourn - er say, give me Je - sus,

Give me . Je - sus, give me Je - sus,

You may have all this world, give me Je - sus.

*Original phrase, "In that morning"

28. Give Me Joy in My Heart

Traditional

Traditional

1 Give me joy in my heart, keep me prais - ing,_____ Give me
2 Give me peace in my heart, keep me lov - ing,_____ Give me
3 Give me love in my heart, keep me serv - ing,_____ Give me

joy in my heart, I pray, Give me joy in my heart, keep me
peace in my heart, I pray, Give me peace in my heart, keep me
love in my heart, I pray, Give me love in my heart, keep me

prais - ing, Keep me prais - ing till the break of day:
lov - ing, Keep me lov - ing till the break of day:
serv - ing, Keep me serv - ing till the break of day:

Refrain

Sing Ho - san - na! Sing ho - san - na! Sing ho-

san - na to the King of kings! Sing Ho - san -

na! Sing ho - san - na! Sing ho - san - na to the King!

From Colin Hodgetts' *Sing True.* Used by permission of the Religious Education Press, Oxford, England.

29. God's Golden Sunshine

Carolyn McDade

Carolyn McDade

Stanza

1 I've got God's gold-en sun-shine a-shin-ing in my win-dow;
warm sum-mer breez-es a-blow-ing in my win-dow;

I've got God's gold-en sun-shine in my soul. I've got God's gold-en
I've got warm sum-mer breez-es in my soul. I've got warm sum-mer

sun-shine a-shin-ing in my win-dow, God's gold-en sun-shine is
breez-es a-blow-ing in my win-dow; Warm sum-mer breez-es are

shin-ing in my soul. Sing-ing Hal-le-lu - Hal-le-lu-jah,
blow-ing in my soul.

Hal-le-lu-jah. Sing-ing Hal-le-lu - Hal-le-lu-jah, Hal-le-lu-

jah. 2 I've got jah. 3 I've got the love of free-dom, of

free-dom in my spir-it, I've got the love of free-dom in my

soul. I've got the love of free-dom, of free-dom in my

spir-it, I've got the love of free-dom, in my soul. Sing-ing

CODA

jah. 4 Gon - na stand and sing life's prais - es, life's prais - es in my spir - it; Gon - na stand and sing life's prais - es in my soul.

Gon - na stand and sing life's prais - es, life's prais - es in my spir - it; Gon - na stand and sing life's prais - es in my soul. Sing - ing

Hal - le - lu - Hal - le - lu - jah, Hal - le - lu - jah, Sing - ing Hal - le - lu - Hal - le - lu - jah, Hal - le - lu - jah.

Fine last time

5 I've got a long - ing for peace, for peace in my spir - it. Got a long - ing for peace in my soul. I've got a long - ing for peace, for peace in my spir - it, Got a long - ing for peace in my soul. Sing - ing

30. God, Who Stretched the Spangled Heavens

Catherine C. Arnott (b.1917)

HOLY MANNA from *Southern Harmony*, setting by O. S., 1977

1 God, who stretched the span-gled heav- ens In - fi - nite in time and place,
2 We have con-quered worlds un-dreamed of Since the child-hood of our race,
3 As Thy new ho - ri - zons beck - on, Fa - ther, give us strength to be,

Flung the suns in burn-ing ra - diance Through the si - lent fields of space,
Known the ec - sta - sy of wing - ing Through un-chart-ed realms of space,
Chil - dren of cre - a - tive pur - pose, Serv - ing man and hon'r-ing Thee,

We Thy chil-dren, in Thy like-ness, Share in - ven - tive pow'rs with Thee;
Probed the se - crets of the at - om, Yield-ing un - im - ag - ined pow'r
Till our dreams are rich with mean-ing, Each en - deav-or, Thy de - sign

Great Cre - a - tor, still cre - a - ting, Teach us what we yet may be.
Fac - ing us with life's de-struc - tion Or our most tri - um-phant hour.
Great Cre - a - tor, lead us on - ward Till our work is one with Thine.

Tune used by permission from *Contemporary Worship Hymns*, prepared by Inter-Lutheran Commission on Worship for Provisional Use.

31. God's Family

Patricia Shelly

Patricia Shelly

Refrain

All grown-ups, all chil-dren, all moth-ers, all fa-thers are
sis-ters and broth-ers in the fam-'ly of God.

1 I am a per-son, God made me spe-cial.
2 So man-y chil-dren, all of them diff-'rent.
3 God has a fam-'ly with man-y peo-ple:

You are a per-son and you're spe-cial too.
God gave each per-son his own thing to do.
Grown-ups and chil-dren who love God to-day.

We have our fam-'lies and friends we can play with;
All of God's chil-dren are sis-ters and broth-ers.
We get to-geth-er to care for each oth-er to

There are so man-y good things we can do.
I know God loves me and God loves you too.
wor-ship and learn how to fol-low God's way.

32. He Has Arisen, Alleluia!

Original text (Swahili): Bernhard Kyamanywa
English: Howard S. Olson, 1969
German: U.S. Leupold, 1969
Note*

Haya tune, Tanzania
Harmony, O. S.

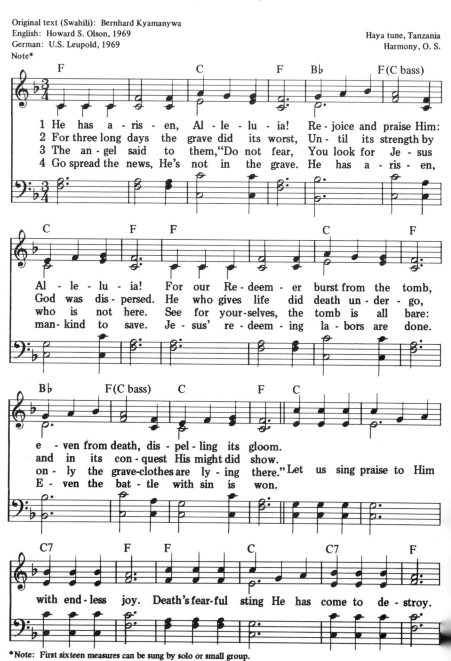

1 He has a - ris - en, Al - le - lu - ia! Re - joice and praise Him:
2 For three long days the grave did its worst, Un - til its strength by
3 The an - gel said to them, "Do not fear, You look for Je - sus
4 Go spread the news, He's not in the grave. He has a - ris - en,

Al - le - lu - ia! For our Re - deem - er burst from the tomb,
God was dis - persed. He who gives life did death un - der - go,
who is not here. See for your-selves, the tomb is all bare:
man - kind to save. Je - sus' re - deem - ing la - bors are done.

e - ven from death, dis - pel - ling its gloom.
and in its con - quest His might did show.
on - ly the grave-clothes are ly - ing there." Let us sing praise to Him
E - ven the bat - tle with sin is won.

with end - less joy. Death's fear-ful sting He has come to de - stroy.

*Note: First sixteen measures can be sung by solo or small group.

From *Cantate Domino*, 1974 by permission of The Lutheran World Federation, Geneva.

Our sins for-giv - ing, Al - le - lu - ia! Je-sus is liv - ing, Al - le - lu - ia!

Swahili:

1 Mfuranini, Halleluya, Mkombozi amefufuka.
Amefufuka, Halleluya, Msifuni sasa yu hai.
Tumwimbie sote kwa furaha. Yesu ametoka kaburini.
Kashinda kifo, Halleluya, Halleluya, yesu yu hai.

2 Amefufuka Mkombozi, Halleluya, tushangilie.
Nguvu za mwovu ameshinda. Ametuondoa kufani.
Tumwimbiesote . . . .

3 Malaika aliwaambia Wanawake, "Msiogope.
Sasa kaburi lip tupu. Kwani Yesu amefufuka."
Tumwimbiesote . . . .

4 Amebatilisha Shetani. Amewaletea wokovu.
Kwa hiyo ninyi mtangaze, Ni hakika, Yesu yu hai.'
Tumwimbiesote . . . .

German:

1 Er ist erstanden, Halleluja. Jauchzt ihm und singet. Halleluja.
Denn unser Heiland hat triumphiert, all seine feind' gefangen er fuhrt.
Lasst uns frohlocken vor unserem Gott, der uns erlöset vom ewigen tod.
Sünd ist vergeben, Halleluja. Jesus bringt leben, Haleluja.

2 Er war begraben drei Tage lang, ihm sei auf ewig Lob, Preis und Dank;
doch die Gewalt des Tods ist zerstört; selig ist, wer zu Jesus gehört.
Lasst uns frohlocken . . . .

3 Der Engel sagte: "Fürchtet euch nicht! Ihr suchet Jesus, er ist hier nicht.
Seht— die Stätte, wo er einst lag: er ist erstanden, wie er gesagt."
Lasst uns frohlocken . . . .

4 Geht und verkündigt, dass Jesus lebt, er lebt in allem, was lebt und webt.
Was Gott geboten, ist nun vollbracht, Christus hat's Leben wiedergebracht.
Lasst uns frohlocken . . . .

33. He Who Dwells in the Shelter of the Most High

Psalm 91

Joseph Gelineau

1 He who dwells in the shelter of the Most High,
2 It is He who will free you from the snare
3 You will not fear the terror of the night,
4 A thousand may fall at your side,
5 Your eyes have only to look,

and a - bides in the shade of the Al - mighty,
of the fowler who seeks to des - troy you,
nor the arrow that flies by day
ten thousand fall at your right,
to see how the wicked are re - paid,

says to the Lord: "My refuge,
He will con - ceal you with His pinions
nor the plague that prowls in the darkness
you, it will never ap - proach;
you who have said: 'Lord, my refuge!'

my stronghold, my God in whom I trust!"
and under - His wings you will find refuge.
nor the scourge that lays waste at noon.
His faithfulness is buckler and shield.
and have made the Most High your dwelling.

Guidelines for singing. One stressed syllable occurs with rigid regularity at the beginning of each measure. Syllables in between the pulse are sung with a natural rhythm. It is helpful to play the pulse in each introductory measure on an instrument, which can be used throughout.

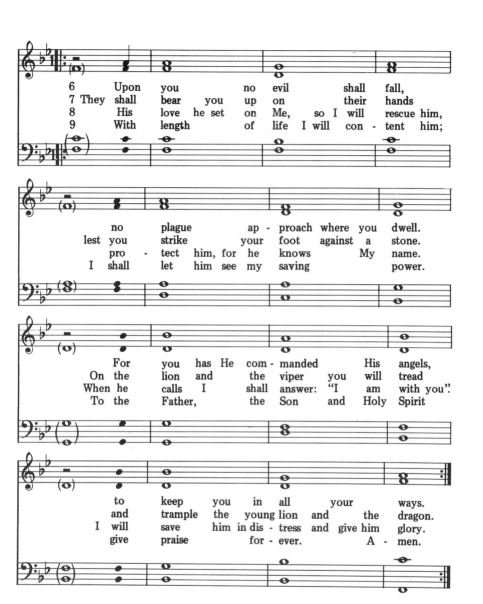

6 Upon you no evil shall fall,
7 They shall bear you up on their hands
8 His love he set on Me, so I will rescue him,
9 With length of life I will con - tent him;

no plague ap - proach where you dwell.
lest you strike your foot against a stone.
pro - tect him, for he knows My name.
I shall let him see my saving power.

For you has He com - manded His angels,
On the lion and the viper you will tread
When he calls I shall answer: "I am with you".
To the Father, the Son and Holy Spirit

to keep you in all your ways.
and trample the young lion and the dragon.
I will save him in dis - tress and give him glory.
give praise for - ever. A - men.

34. He's Got the Whole World in His Hands

Negro spiritual

Negro spiritual

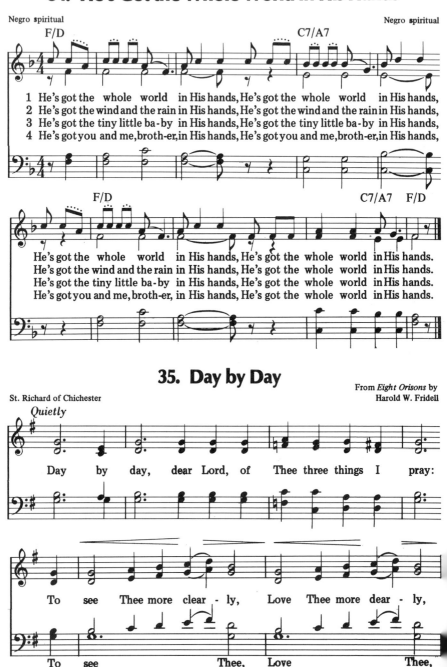

1 He's got the whole world in His hands, He's got the whole world in His hands,
2 He's got the wind and the rain in His hands, He's got the wind and the rain in His hands,
3 He's got the tiny little ba-by in His hands, He's got the tiny little ba-by in His hands,
4 He's got you and me, broth-er, in His hands, He's got you and me, broth-er, in His hands,

He's got the whole world in His hands, He's got the whole world in His hands.
He's got the wind and the rain in His hands, He's got the whole world in His hands.
He's got the tiny little ba-by in His hands, He's got the whole world in His hands.
He's got you and me, broth-er, in His hands, He's got the whole world in His hands.

35. Day by Day

From *Eight Orisons* by
Harold W. Fridell

St. Richard of Chichester

Quietly

Day by day, dear Lord, of Thee three things I pray:

To see Thee more clear-ly, Love Thee more dear-ly,

To see Thee, Love Thee,

Fol - low Thee more near - ly, Day by day.

36. Every Time I Feel the Spirit

Negro spiritual
Refrain

Negro spiritual
Arr. by O. S.

Ev - 'ry time I feel the Spir - it mov - ing in my heart

I will pray; I will pray.

1 Up - on the moun - tain
Looked all a - round me,
2 Oh, I have sor - rows
But my God leads me,

when my Lord spoke, out of His mouth came fire and smoke;
it looked so fine, I asked my Lord if all were mine.
and I have heart And I have heart - aches here be - low;
I'm in His care, And I can feel Him ev - 'ry - where.

37. Happy Is the Name of the Lord

Henry Unrau

Henry Unrau

1 Hap-py is the name of the Lord. Hap-py is the
2 Free-dom is the name of the Lord. Free-dom is the

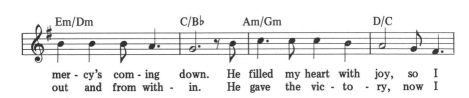

name of the Lord. His love knows no bounds, and His
name of the Lord. He set me free from sin from with-

mer-cy's com-ing down. He filled my heart with joy, so I
out and from with-in. He gave the vic-to-ry, now I

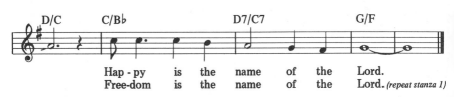

spread it all a-round. Hap-py is the name of the Lord.
owe my life to Him. Free-dom is the name of the Lord.

D/C   C/Bb   D7/C7   G/F

Hap-py is the name of the Lord.
Free-dom is the name of the Lord. *(repeat stanza 1)*

38. I Feel the Winds of God Today

Jessie Adams, (1863-)   Norwegian folk melody

1 I feel the winds of God to-day; To-day my sail I lift,
2 It is the wind of God that dries My vain re-gret-ful tears,
3 If ev-er I for-get Thy love And how that love was shown,

Though heav-y oft with drench-ing spray, And torn with man-y a rift;
Un-til with brav-er thoughts shall rise The pur-er, bright-er years;
Lift high the blood-red flag a-bove: It bears Thy name a-lone.

If hope but light the wa-ter's crest And Christ my bark will use,
If cast on shores of self-ish ease Or pleas-ure I should be,
Great Pi-lot of my on-ward way, Thou wilt not let me drift;

I'll seek the seas at His be-hest, And brave an-oth-er cruise.
Lord, let me feel Thy fresh-'ning breeze, And I'll put back to sea.
I feel the winds of God to-day, To-day my sail I lift.

39. I Have Decided to Follow Jesus

Alternate words
by James E. Byrne

Traditional

1. I have de-cid-ed to fol-low Je-sus, I have de-cid-ed to fol-low Je-sus, I have de-cid-ed to fol-low Je-sus,
2. The world be-hind me, the cross be-fore me; The world be-hind me, the cross be-fore me, the cross be-fore me,
3. Tho' none go with me, I still will fol-low, Tho' none go with me, I still will fol-low, I still will fol-low,
4. Will you de-cide now to fol-low Je-sus? Will you de-cide now to fol-low Je-sus? to fol-low Je-sus,

No turn-ing back, no turn-ing back.

Alternate words:

1. We have decided to follow Jesus,
   No turning back,

2. For He has called us to be His people,
   No turning back.

3. He is among us to heal our sorrow,
   And bring us joy.

4. He goes before us unto His Father,
   To lead us home.

5. He sends His Spirit to be our comfort,
   Till He returns.

6. Oh come be with us, our risen Savior!
   And be our joy!

40. I Will Extol My God, My King

Psalm 145: 1 - 3
Trans. by Eunice L. DeMiller

Casiodoro Cárdenas

I will ex-tol my God, my King, and for-ev-er
bless His ho-ly name. Now and for-ev-er I will
bless Him, I will sing the prais-es of the Lord.
I will bless His name, O God, my King, now and for-
ev-er I will bless Him. O how great is the Lord,
and wor-thy of all praise and a-do-ra-tion.
O how mag-ni-fi-cent is God's great-ness;
I will sing the prais-es of the Lord.

Teex-al-ta-ré, mi-Dios, mi Rey, y ben-de-ci
ré tu nom-bre e-ter-na-men tey pa-ra
siem-pre; ca-da dí-a Te ben-de-ci-ré,
y a la-ba-ré tu nom-bre e-ter-na-
men-tey pa-ra siem-pre, Gran-de es Je-ho-vá,
y dig-no de su-pre-ma a-la-ban-za;
y su gran-de-zaes i-nes-cru-ta-ble;
ca-da dí-a te ben-de-ci-ré.

Published in *Cantad al Señor Cántico Nuevo* edited by Jorge Maldonado Rivera. Permission requested from Iglesia del Pacto Evangélico en el Ecuador. English words copyright 1978 by Mennonite World Conference, Lombard, IL 60148.

41. I Will Sing, I Will Sing

Max Dyer   Max Dyer

Liltingly

1 I will sing, I will sing a song un-to the Lord.
2 Al-le-lu, al-le-lu-ia, glo-ry to the Lord.

I will sing, I will sing a song un-to the Lord.
Al-le-lu, al-le-lu-ia, glo-ry to the Lord.

I will sing, I will sing a song un-to the Lord.
Al-le-lu, al-le-lu-ia, glo-ry to the Lord.

Al-le-lu-ia, glo-ry to the Lord.
Al-le-lu-ia, glo-ry to the Lord.

Optional stanzas:

3 We will come, we will come as one before the Lord.
   Alleluia, glory to the Lord.

4 They that sow, they that sow in tears shall reap in joy.
   Alleluia, glory to the Lord.

5 In His name, in His name we have the victory.
   Alleluia, glory to the Lord.

Note: This song is most effectively sung without any instrumental accompaniment, but with light clapping (finger tips of one hand on palm of another). Suggested rhythm: ♩ ♫♩ ♫♩ , etc.

42. I Will Sing of the Mercies of the Lord

Psalm 89:1   Traditional

43. I Will Sing unto the Lord

Note: These three choruses can be sung at the same time in various combinations.

44. I Wish I Could Sing

Trans. by Ruby Wiebe

Zaire
Congolese spiritual
Arr. by Ruby Wiebe

I wish I could sing, as an - gels can sing.
Könnte sing - en ich wie En - gel so schön

I wish I could fly, as an - gels can fly.
Könnte flie gen ich wie En - gel so schön!

I'd like to soar with hea - ven - ly wings like oth - er an - gels,
Sing -end auf-schwing-en nür - de ich mich, bring - en dem Schöpf-er

Then I'd sing a hea - ven - ly song. I'd sing all day long.
ganz inig - lich ein nue - es Lied, ein lieb - lich - es Lied.

Males:
Hal - le - lu - jah, sing praise to God. Hal - le
Lob - prei - set Gott!

Females:

Males:

Females:
lu - jah, sing praise to God. Hal - le - lu - jah,
Lob - prei - set Gott!

Males:

Females:
All:
sing praise to God. Ho - san - na, ho - san - na.
Lob - prei - set Gott! Ho - sian - na, ho - sian - na.

Drum Beat:

45. In the Morning, O God

(Prayer)

Marji Hazen

Marji Hazen
Accomp., O. S.

1 In the morn-ing, O God, do I lift up mine eyes in
2 In the si-lence O God, would I o-pen mine ears to

prayer to Thee. With Thy help would I purge all de-
hear Thy voice. Here I wait. O my God, help me

sire from my heart save de-sire of Thee. Lead me, O
fol-low what-ev-er shall be Thy choice. Use me, O

God, for will-ing-ly now would I seek Thy face;
God, for will-ing-ly now would I be Thy hands;

Hear me, O God, for here in this dawn do I call Thy name.
Use me, O God, that the day may be Thine and the joy there-of.

46. I'm Gonna Sing

Negro spiritual

Negro spiritual

I'm gon-na sing* when the Spir-it says, sing,* I'm gon-na

sing* when the Spir-it says sing;* I'm gon-na sing* when the Spir-it says

sing* And o-bey the Spir-it of the Lord.

*Substitute shout, preach, pray.

47. Is There Anybody Here Like Mary A-Weeping

WEEPING MARY
American folk hymn

Stanza 1: Traditional American folk hymn
Stanzas 2, 3: Wm. B Schmidgall (b. 1919)

Harmony: Gerre Hancock (b. 1934)

1 Is there an-y-bod-y here like Ma-ry a-weep-ing,
2 Is there an-y-bod-y here like Pe-ter a-sink-ing,
3 Is there an-y-bod-y here like Tho-mas a-doubt-ing,

Call on my Je-sus and He'll draw nigh. Is there
Call on my Je-sus and He'll draw nigh. Is there
Call on my Je-sus and He'll draw nigh. Is there

an-y-bod-y here like Ma-ry a-weep-ing,
an-y-bod-y here like Pe-ter a-sink-ing,
an-y-bod-y here like Tho-mas a-doubt-ing,

Refrain

Call on my Je-sus and He'll draw nigh.
Call on my Je-sus and He'll draw nigh.
Call on my Je-sus and He'll draw nigh. Glo-ry, glo-ry,

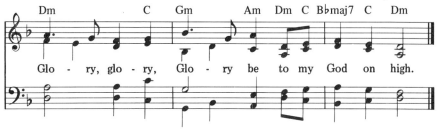

Dm		C	Gm		Am Dm C B♭maj7 C Dm

Glo - ry, glo - ry, Glo - ry be to my God on high.

48. I Want Jesus to Walk with Me

Traditional
Arr. by John F. Wilson

Spiritual

Dm A7 Dm		A7/G7	Dm Am Dm
/Cm /G7 /Cm			/Cm /Gm /Cm

1 ____ I want Je - sus to walk with me; ____ I want
2 ____ In my tri - als, Lord, walk with me; ____ In my
3 When I'm in trou - ble, Lord, walk with me; When I'm in

F/E♭ C/B♭ F/E♭		A7 B♭ A7		Dm/Cm	Gm C7
		/G7 /A♭ /G7			/Fm /B♭7

Je - sus to walk with me; ____ All a - long my pil - grim
tri - als, Lord, walk with me; ____ When my heart is al - most
trou - ble, Lord, walk with me; ____ When my head is bowed in

Dm/Cm	B♭/A♭ C7/B♭7	Dm B♭ Gm7	A7/G7	Dm Gm Dm
		/Cm /A♭ /Fm7		/Cm /Fm /Cm

jour - ney, Lord, I want Je - sus ____ to walk with me. ____
break - ing, Lord, I want Je - sus ____ to walk with me. ____
sor - row, Lord, I want Je - sus ____ to walk with me. ____

49. In Christ There Is No East or West

John Oxenham (1852-1941)
Based on Galatians 3:28

Negro melody adapted by
Harry T. Burleigh (1866-1949)

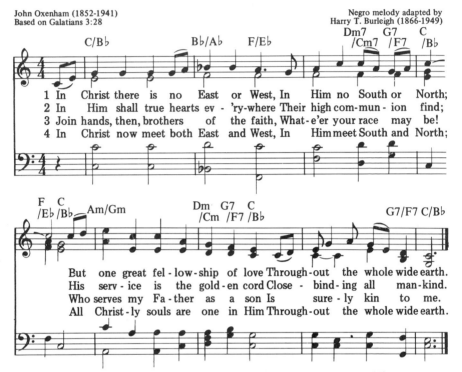

1 In Christ there is no East or West, In Him no South or North;
2 In Him shall true hearts ev - 'ry-where Their high com-mun - ion find;
3 Join hands, then, brothers of the faith, What-e'er your race may be!
4 In Christ now meet both East and West, In Him meet South and North;

But one great fel-low-ship of love Through-out the whole wide earth.
His serv-ice is the gold-en cord Close - bind-ing all man-kind.
Who serves my Fa-ther as a son Is sure - ly kin to me.
All Christ-ly souls are one in Him Through-out the whole wide earth.

Words used by permission from *Sing!* published by Fortress Press, Philadelphia, 1969.

50. Jesus, Jesus

Alf Siemens and Tom Graff

T. Ravenscroft, 1635

1 Al - le - lu - ia! Sing for joy and cel - e - brate, He
2 Je - sus, Sav - ior, in a lone - ly world You love us.
3 Je - sus, Teach-er, show-ing us to love all peo - ple,

comes a - gain in truth and glo - ry, Je - sus is Lord.
God who made us, give us cour - age, Christ give us strength.
Love our neigh-bors as our-selves, for Christ gives us peace.

From *The Joyful Round*, copyright, Grapple Press, Vancouver, B.C., Canada.

51. Jesus, Loving Lord
(An Indian Blessing)

Original text: Hindi

Gazar

Je - sus— lov - ing Lord; Je - sus,— strength and— stay, in— Your mer - cy bless us all and keep us night and day.

Ye - shu— su - pri - ya, Ye - shu— a - shra - ye. Ye - shu pri - ya ta - ra - ka, sa - ha - ya ho - ma - la.

52. Kyrie Eleison

Original text: Greek

Herbert Beuerle, 1967

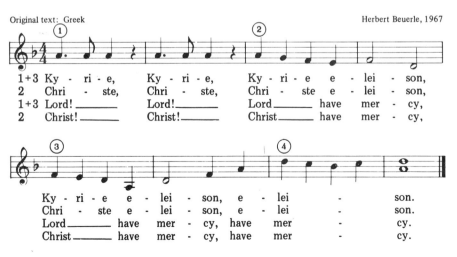

1+3 Ky - ri - e, Ky - ri - e, Ky - ri - e e - lei - son,
2 Chri - ste, Chri - ste, Chri - ste e - lei - son,
1+3 Lord!____ Lord!____ Lord____ have mer - cy,
2 Christ!____ Christ!____ Christ____ have mer - cy,

Ky - ri - e e - lei - son, e - lei - son.
Chri - ste e - lei - son, e - lei - son.
Lord____ have mer - cy, have mer - cy.
Christ____ have mer - cy, have mer - cy.

53. Let There Be Peace on Earth

Sy Miller and Jill Jackson

Sy Miller and Jill Jackson

Let there be peace on earth And let it be-gin with me;—

Let there be peace on earth, The peace that was meant to be.—

— With God as our Fa-ther, Bro-thers all are we.
(All one fa-mi-ly.)*

Let me walk with my bro-ther In per-fect har-mo-ny.—
(us) (each oth-er)

*Optional words in parentheses.

54. Let the Nations Give You Thanks
(Te Den Gracias)

Source of text unknown
Tr. by Sara Claassen

P. Eduardo de Zayas

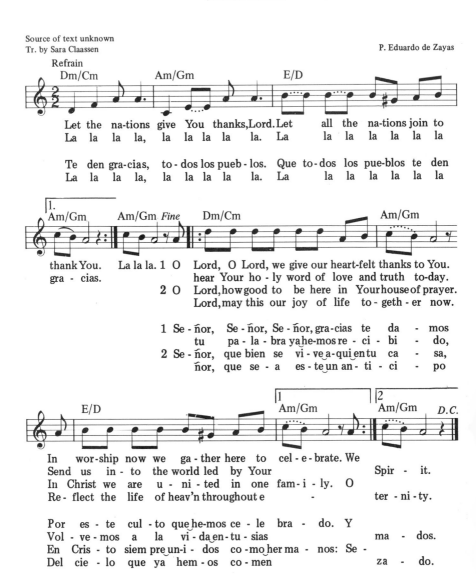

Refrain

Let the na-tions give You thanks, Lord. Let all the na-tions join to
La la la la, la la la la la. La la la la la la la la

Te den gra-cias, to-dos los pueb-los. Que to-dos los pue-blos te den
La la la la, la la la la la. La la la la la la la

Fine

thank You. La la la. 1 O Lord, O Lord, we give our heart-felt thanks to You.
gra-cias.   hear Your ho-ly word of love and truth to-day.
    2 O Lord, how good to be here in Your house of prayer.
      Lord, may this our joy of life to-geth-er now.

1 Se-ñor, Se-ñor, Se-ñor, gra-cias te da-mos,
    tu pa-la-bra ya he-mos re-ci-bi-do,
2 Se-ñor, que bien se vi-ve a-quien tu ca-sa,
    ñor, que se-a es-te un an-ti-ci-po

D.C.

In wor-ship now we ga-ther here to cel-e-brate. We
Send us in-to the world led by Your Spir-it.
In Christ we are u-ni-ted in one fam-i-ly. O
Re-flect the life of heav'n throughout e-ter-ni-ty.

Por es-te cul-to que he-mos ce-le bra-do. Y
Vol-ve-mos a la vi-da en-tu-sias ma-dos.
En Cris-to siem pre un-i-dos co-mo her ma-nos: Se-
Del cie-lo que ya hem-os co-men za-do.

55. Let Us Break Bread Together

Negro spiritual
Arr. by J. Harold Moyer

Negro spiritual

1 Let us break bread to-geth-er on our knees
2 Let us drink wine to-geth-er on our knees (yes on our knees).
3 Let us praise God to-geth-er on our knees

Let us break bread to-geth-er on our knees
Let us drink wine to-geth-er on our knees (yes on our knees).
Let us praise God to-geth-er on our knees

When I fall on my knees with my face to the ris-ing sun,

O Lord, have mer-cy on me (on me).

56. Let Us Give Thanks

Tom Graff

T. Ravenscroft, 1635

Let us give thanks to the Lord, for His good - ness, for the joy in liv - ing, has come from His love.

From *The Joyful Round,* copyright, Grapple Press, Vancouver, B.C., Canada

57. Burden Down

(As Sung at Lincoln School, Marion, Alabama)

Traditional

Traditional
Arr. by Olive J. Williams

1 Bur - den down, Lord, Bur - den down, Lord,
2 Won - der will my sis - ter know me,
3 Won - der will my bro - ther know me,   Since I lay my bur - den
4 Bur - den down, Lord, Bur - den down, Lord,

down.   Bur-den down, Lord, Bur-den down, Lord, Since I lay my bur-den down.

From *In Harmony*, published by the United Christian Youth Movement.

58. Let Us with a Gladsome Mind

Original text based on Ps. 136: John Milton (1608-1674)
German: Johann Christoph Hampe
Spanish: F.J. Pagura

Chinese traditional chant

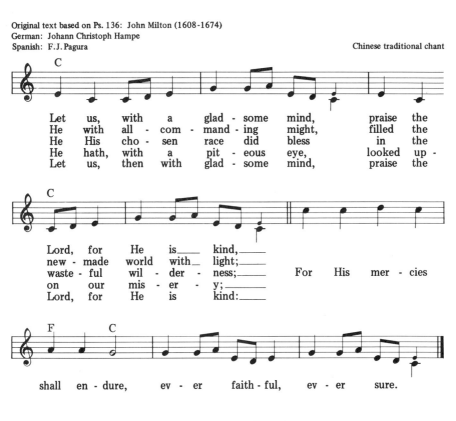

Let us, with a glad - some mind, praise the
He with all - com - mand - ing might, filled the
He His cho - sen race did bless in the
He hath, with a pit - eous eye, looked up -
Let us, then with glad - some mind, praise the

Lord, for He is___ kind,___
new - made world with_ light;___
waste - ful wil - der - ness;___   For His mer - cies
on our mis - er - y;___
Lord, for He is kind:___

shall en - dure, ev - er faith - ful, ev - er sure.

German:

Brüder, macht die Herzen weit,
  euren Mund zum Lob bereit!
Gottes Güte, Gottes Treu
  sind an jedem Morgenneu.

Gottes Hand erschafft die Welt,
  Finsternis sein Wort erhellt.
Gottes Güte . . . .

Je und je sein Segen war
  über der erwählten Schar.
Gottes Gute . . . .

Und sein Blick aus Himmelshöh'n
  hat das Elend angeseh'n.
Gottes Gute . . . .

Macht darum die Herzen weit,
  euern Mund zum Lob bereit!
Gottes Gute . . . .

Spanish:

Al Señor, con alegría,
  suban nuestras melodías,
Porque inmensa es su bondad,
  firme por la eternidad.

A su voz omnipotente
  fué la luz resplandeciente,
Porque inmensa es . . . .

Dió a su pueblo bendiciones
  en sus peregrinaciones,
Porque inmensa es . . . .

El con ojos paternales
  se apiadó de nuestros males,
Porque inmensa es . . . .

Demos pués, con alegría,
  gloria a Dios, en este día.
Porque inmensa es . . . .

From *Cantate Domino*, 1974, by permission of the World Council of Churches, Geneva.

59. Like David the Shepherd, I Sing

Anonymous, Spanish
Trans. by editors of *International Songbook*

Traditional

1 //Si el Espíritu de Dios
se mueve en mi,
yo canto como David.//
//Yo canto, yo canto,
yo canto como David.//

2 //Si el Espíritu de Dios
se mueve en mi,
yo oro, como David.//
//Yo oro, yo oro,
yo oro como David.//

3 //Si el Espíritu de Dios
se mueve en mi.
Yo bailo como David.//
//Yo bailo, yo bailo,
yo bailo como David.//

4 //Si el Espíritu de Dios
se mueve en mi,
yo alabo como David.//
//Yo alabo, yo alabo,
yo alabo como David.//

60. Living Stones

Marilyn Houser Hamm

Marilyn Houser Hamm

1 ♪ Be - hold the Lord has called His chil - dren His own,
2 Be - hold what a plea - sant and beau - ti - ful sight
3 ♪ Weak and yet strong with the Spir - it to lead, We

And with our ris - en Lord, we are liv - ing stones,
Are those who have come from their dark - ness to
are mold - ed to one - ness, a grow - ing seed,

Light as Liv - ing stones, liv - ing stones,

to build up the king - dom, liv - ing stones,

♪ Be - hold the Lord has called His chil - dren His own,
How hap - py are those come from dark - ness to light,
♪ Mold - ed to one - ness, a grow - ing seed,

to build up the king - dom, liv - ing stones.

61. Lonesome Valley

Collected in Southern Highlands by
Gladys V. Jameson (b. 1889) in 1932

Traditional
Arr. by Don Ross

*This may also be sung by the congregation in unison with or without instrumental accompaniment.

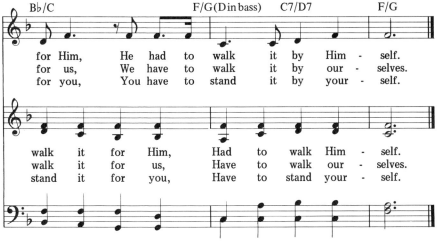

Bb/C   F/G(D in bass)   C7/D7   F/G

for Him,   He had to walk   it by Him - self.
for us,   We have to walk   it by our - selves.
for you,   You have to stand   it by your - self.

walk it for Him,   Had to walk Him - self.
walk it for us,   Have to walk our - selves.
stand it for you,   Have to stand your - self.

62. Hallelujah

Palestinian folk song

Very fast
Gm/Fm   Dm/Cm   Gm/Fm

Hal - le - lu - jah, hal - le - lu - jah, hal - le - lu - jah, hal - le - lu!

Dm/Cm   Gm/Fm

Hal - le - lu - jah, hal - le - lu - jah, hal - le - lu - jah, hal - le - lu!

Hal - le - lu - jah, hal - le - lu!   Hal - le - lu - jah, hal - le - lu!

Dm/Cm   Gm/Fm

Hal - le - lu - jah, hal - le - lu - jah, hal - le - lu - jah, hal - le - lu!

From *The Good Times Songbook*, edited by James Leisy. Abingdon Press, 1974.

63. Lord and Master, We Beseech Thee

(Graduation Hymn, Also Suitable for Other Occasions)

Anne Marie Warkentin

George Wiebe

1 Lord and Mas-ter, we be-seech Thee, To be with us through this day;
3 E - ven now our path lies hid - den, But to fol - low is our aim;

Let us feel Thy ho - ly pre-sence, Now and on our fu - ture way.
Give us hum-ble hearts in ser - vice, That we glo - ri - fy Thy name.

Melody in tenor

2 Thou hast been our help and guid-ance, Ev -'ry day through-out the year;
4 Now to Thee be praise and hon - or, For the way that Thou hast led;

Grant that e - ver in the fu - ture, We may fol - low with - out fear.
And we trust Thee for the fu - ture, As our un - known path we tread.

64. Lord Christ, the Father's Mighty Son

Brian Wren, 1965

Peter Cutts, 1965

In unison

1 Lord Christ, the Fa - ther's might - y Son, Whose
2 To make us one Your prayers were said, To
3 O Christ, for - give us, make us new! We
4 We will not ques - tion or re - fuse The

work up - on the cross was done all men to re - ceive, Make
make us one You broke the bread, for all to re - ceive; Its
know the best that we can do will noth - ing a - chieve, And,
way You work, the means You choose, the pat - tern You weave, But

all our scat - ter'd chur - ches one, that the world may be - lieve.
pie - ces scat - ter us in - stead: how can oth - ers be - lieve?
hum - bled, bring our prayers to You, that the world may be - lieve.
re - con - cile, our war - ring views, that the world may be - lieve.

65. Lord of Light Whose Name Outshineth

TON - Y - BOTEL
Welsh hymn melody

Howell Elvet Lewis, 1916

Thomas John Williams (1869-1944)

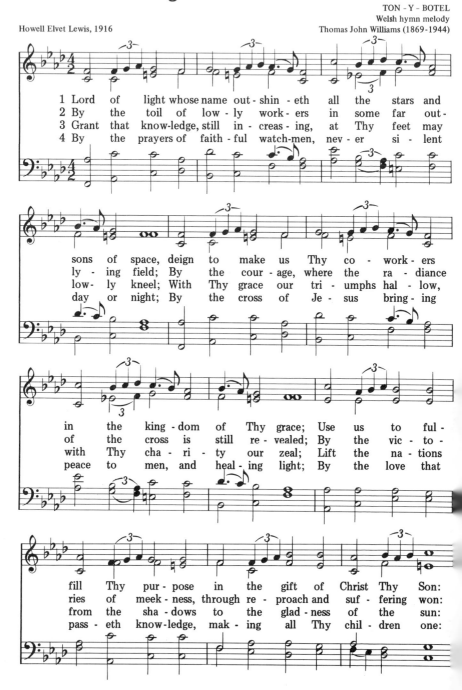

1 Lord of light whose name out-shin - eth all the stars and
2 By the toil of low - ly work-ers in some far out-
3 Grant that know-ledge, still in - creas - ing, at Thy feet may
4 By the prayers of faith - ful watch-men, nev - er si - lent

sons of space, deign to make us Thy co - work - ers
ly - ing field; By the cour - age, where the ra - diance
low - ly kneel; With Thy grace our tri - umphs hal - low,
day or night; By the cross of Je - sus bring - ing

in the king - dom of Thy grace; Use us to ful -
of the cross is still re - vealed; By the vic - to -
with Thy cha - ri - ty our zeal; Lift the na - tions
peace to men, and heal - ing light; By the love that

fill Thy pur - pose in the gift of Christ Thy Son:
ries of meek - ness, through re - proach and suf - fering won:
from the sha - dows to the glad - ness of the sun:
pass - eth know-ledge, mak - ing all Thy chil - dren one:

1-4 Fa - ther, as in high-est hea-ven, so on earth Thy will be done.

66. He Is King of Kings

Negro spiritual

Negro spiritual
Harmony by W. Lawrence Curry

Refrain
D A D D A D

He is King of kings, He is Lord of lords!

Bm A D G D/A A D *Fine*

Je - sus Christ, the first and last, No one works like Him.

Bm A D G D/A A D *D.C.*

1 I know that my Re-deem-er lives,
And by His love sweet bless-ing gives.
2 He builds a plat-form in the air,
And calls the saints from ev-ery-where.
3 O sin - ner, if you will be-lieve,
The grace of the Lord you will re-ceive.

No one works like Him!

67. Lord of the Dance

Sydney Carter

Based on a Shaker tune
Arr. and adapted by Sydney Carter

Lyrics:

1 I danced in the morn-ing when the world was be-gun, And I danced in the moon and the stars and the sun, And I came down from heav-en and I danced on the earth,

2 I danced for the scribe and the Phar-i-see; But they would not dance and they would-n't fol-low Me, I danced for the fish-er-men, for

3 I danced on the Sab-bath and I cured the lame; The ho-ly peo-ple said it was a shame. They whipped and they stripped and they

4 I danced on a Fri-day and the sky turned black It's hard to dance with the dev-il on your back. They bur-ied my bod-y and they

5 They cut me down and I leapt up high I am the life that-'ll nev-er, nev-er die; I'll live in you if you'll

68. Love, Love, Love

Herbert Brokering

Lois Brokering

Loud

1 Love, love, love!
2 Peace, peace, peace!
3 Joy, joy, joy! That's what it's all a - bout! 'Cause God loves us, we
4 Me, me, me!
5 You, you, you!

love each oth - er, Moth - er, fa - ther, sis - ter, broth - er,

Ev - 'ry - bod - y sing and shout 'Cause that's what it's all a -

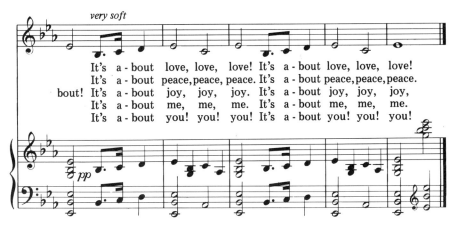

very soft

It's a - bout love, love, love! It's a - bout love, love, love!
It's a - bout peace, peace, peace. It's a - bout peace, peace, peace.
bout! It's a - bout joy, joy, joy. It's a - bout joy, joy, joy,
It's a - bout me, me, me. It's a - bout me, me, me.
It's a - bout you! you! you! It's a - bout you! you! you!

69. Obey My Voice

Jeremiah 7:23

Sheilagh Nowacki

O - bey My voice and I will be your God and ye shall

be My peo - ple. And walk in all the ways I have com -

mand - ed you that it may be well with you and

I will be your God. O - bey My voice and I will be your

God and ye shall be My peo - ple.

70. Many Gifts

Patricia Shelly
Acc. by Dennis Friesen Carper

1 Corinthians 12

There are man - y gifts, but the same

Spir - it. There are man - y works, but the same God. And the

Spir - it gives each as He choos - es, Praise the Lord. Praise

1 Now one has the gift ___ of wis - dom; an -
God. 2 A bod - y has man - y mem - bers, yet
3 Not all are ___ called to be pro - phets; and

oth - er the call - ing to speak.
all work in u - ni - ty.
not all are called to preach.

One the a - bil - i - ty to
The church is the bod - y
But all should aim for the

com - fort; an - oth - er the call - ing to teach.
of Christ: His arms, ears, and eyes, hands and feet.
best gifts — and love is the great - est of these.

There are

71. Many Gifts, One Spirit

Al Carmines

Al Carmines

1 God of change and glo - ry, God of time and space,
2 God of man - y col - ors, God of man - y signs,
3 Fresh - ness of the morn - ing, New - ness of each night,

When we fear the fu - ture Give to us Your grace.
You have made us diff - 'rent, Bless - ings man - y kinds.
You are still cre - at - ing End - less love and light.

In the midst of chang - ing ways Give us still the grace to praise.
As the old ways dis - ap - pear Let Your love cast out our fear.
This we see, as shad - ows part, Man - y gifts from one great heart.

72. Love Song

1 Corinthians 13

Patricia Shelly

Refrain: Love is pa-tient and kind, slow to an-ger. Love de-lights in truth.

There is noth-ing that love can-not face and love en-dures, love en-dures.

1 If I speak in tongues of men or an-gels, and have no
2 If I have the gift of pro-phecy, and know
3 Are there pro-phets— their work—will be o-ver, are there
4 There are three things——— that last for-ev-er out of

love and have no love, I am a nois-y gong or clang-ing
ev-'ry hid-den truth. Or have faith strong e-nough to move
tongues, their voice will cease. Is there know-ledge——it too will
all I'm sing-ing of. There is faith——————— and hope and

cym-bal with-out love, with-out love.
moun-tains: with-out love what is the use?
pass a-way, on-ly love lives e-ter-nal-ly.
char-i-ty, but the great-est of these is love.

73. My Lord, What a Mornin

Negro spiritual

Negro spiritual
Arr. by J. Rosamond Johnson

hear the trum-pet sound,
hear the sin - ner moan, To wake the na-tions un - der ground,
hear the Christ-ians shout,

Look-in' to my God's right hand, When the stars be-gin to fall. My

Lord, what a morn-in', My Lord, what a morn-in', My Lord, what a

morn-in', When the stars be-gin to fall, When the stars be-gin to

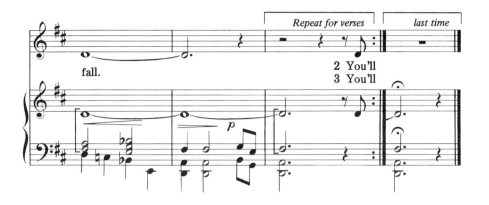

Repeat for verses *last time*

fall.

2 You'll
3 You'll

74. Alleluia

Anon.
Arr. by Betty Pulkingham

| G | C | Am |

1 Al - le - lu - ia, Al - le - lu - ia, Al - le -
2 How I love Him, How I love Him, How I
3 Bless-ed Je - sus, Bless-ed Je - sus, Bless-ed
4 My Re - deem - er, My Re - deem - er, My Re -
5 Je - sus is Lord! Je - sus is Lord! Je - sus
6 Al - le - lu - ia, Al - le - lu - ia, Al - le -

D 1 C G 2 C G

lu - ia, Al - le - lu - ia, Al - le - lu - ia.
love Him, How I love Him, How I love Him.
Je - sus, Bless-ed Je - sus, Bless-ed Je - sus.
deem - er, My Re - deem - er, My Re - deem - er.
is Lord! Je - sus is Lord! Je - sus is Lord!
lu - ia, Al - le - lu - ia, Al - le - lu - ia.

75. Mighty God, to Thy Dear Name

Original text (Norwegian): Perrer Dass (1640-1707)
English and German trans.: Eivind Berggrav, 1951-2

Norwegian folk song
Harmony, O.S.

1. Might-y God, to Thy dear name be giv-en
2 God is God tho' all the earth lay wast-ed;
3 High-est hills and deep-est vales shall van-ish,

high-est praise in all the earth and heav-en.
God is God, tho' all men death had tast-ed.
earth and heav-en both a-like be ban-ished,

All souls dis-tressed,___ all men op-pressed,___ their
While na-tions stum-ble, in dark-ness fum-ble, by
As in the dawn-ing of ev-'ry morn-ing, the

voic-es rais-ing u-nite in prais-ing Thy glo-ry.
stars sur-round-ed count-less a-bound-eth God's har-vest.
sun ap-pear-eth so glo-rious near-eth God's king-dom.

German:

1 Herre Gott, deins teuren Namens Ehre
  Singen Erde und des Himmels Heere.
  Ob Sorgen quälen die müden Seelen,
  Dennoch sie preisen mit frohen Weisen dich, Herre.

2 Gott bleibt Gott, ob alle Welt versänke,
  Gott bleibt Gott, ob Kreatur ertränke.
  Was auch auf Erden Asche mag werden,
  In lichten Hallen dort oben schallen dir Lieder.

3 Hohe Berg und tiefe Täler weichen,
  Erd und Himmel fallen solln desgleichen.
  Die stolzen Zinnen wie Rauch zerrinnen,
  Doch fest wird stehen und nie vergehen dein Name.

76. Our Father, Who Art in Heaven

(The Lord's Prayer)

Traditional

77. May the Lord Grant His Peace

(Benediction Circle-Canon)

Philip K. Clemens

May the Lord grant His peace un - to thee, while we are

May the Lord grant His peace un - to

ab - sent one from the oth - er, May the

thee, while we are ab - sent one from the

Lord grant His peace un - to thee, while we are

oth - er, May the Lord grant His peace un - to

Fine, last time

ab - sent one from the oth - er, May the

thee, while we are ab-sent one from the oth - er. May the

Fine, last time

78. My Soul Doth Magnify the Lord

(Magnificat)

D.T. Niles
Based on Luke 1:46-55

Maluku popular tune
Arr. by Mervyn S. Rosser, 1962
(slightly alt., O.S., 1976)

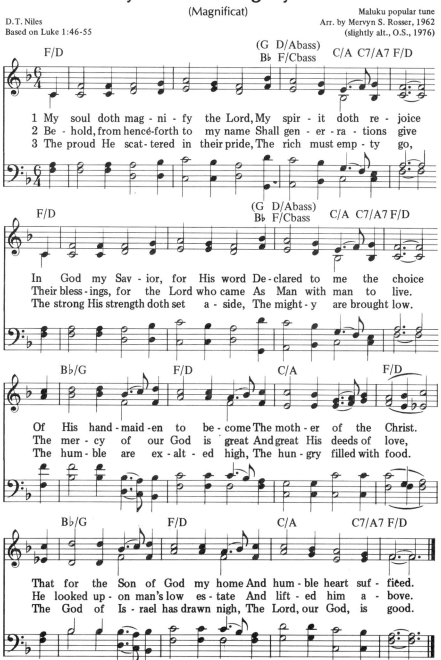

1 My soul doth mag-ni-fy the Lord, My spir-it doth re-joice
2 Be-hold, from hence-forth to my name Shall gen-er-ra-tions give
3 The proud He scat-tered in their pride, The rich must emp-ty go,

In God my Sav-ior, for His word De-clared to me the choice
Their bless-ings, for the Lord who came As Man with man to live.
The strong His strength doth set a-side, The might-y are brought low.

Of His hand-maid-en to be-come The moth-er of the Christ.
The mer-cy of our God is great And great His deeds of love,
The hum-ble are ex-alt-ed high, The hun-gry filled with food.

That for the Son of God my home And hum-ble heart suf-ficed.
He looked up-on man's low es-tate And lift-ed him a-bove.
The God of Is-rael has drawn nigh, The Lord, our God, is good.

Words by permission of the Christian Conference of Asia; tune from the National Christian Council of Indonesia.

79. Now Let Us from This Table Rise

HURSLEY
Arr. from *Grosser Gott, wir loben dich*
From *Katholisches Gesangbuch*, Vienna, 1776

Fred Kaan, (b. 1929)

1 Now let us from this ta - ble rise re - newed in
2 With minds a - lert, up - held by grace, to spread the
3 To fill each hu - man house with love, it is the
4 Then grant us cour - age, Fa - ther God, to choose a -

bod - y, mind, and soul; With Christ we die and
Word in speech and deed, We fol - low in the
sac - ra - ment of care; The work that Christ be -
gain the pil - grim way And help us to ac -

live a - gain, His self - less love has made us whole.
steps of Christ, At one with man in hope and need.
gan to do We hum - bly pledge our - selves to share.
cept with joy The chal - lenge of to - mor - row's day.

Alternate tune: TALLIS' CANON

80. Now the Green Blade Riseth

(Love Is Come Again)

J.M.C. Crum (1872-1958)

Traditional French tune
Harmony, O. S.

1 Now the green blade ris - eth from the bur - ied grain,
2 In the grave they laid Him, Love whom men had slain,
3 Forth He came at Eas - ter, like the ris - en grain,
4 When our hearts are win - try, griev - ing, or in pain,

Wheat that in the dark earth man - y days has lain
Think - ing that __ nev - er He would wake a - gain;
He __ that for three days in the grave had lain.
Thy __ touch can call us back to life a - gain.

Love lives a - gain, that with the dead has been;
Laid in the earth like grain that sleeps un - seen,
Quick from the dead my ris - en Lord is seen;
Fields of our hearts that dead and bare have been;

1-4 Love is come a - gain, like wheat that spring - eth green.

From the *Oxford Book of Carols*. Used by permission of Oxford University Press.

81. O for a Thousand Tongues

Charles Wesley (1707-1788)

LYNGHAM
Thomas Jarman

Joyfully, with movement

1 O for a thou - sand tongues to sing My great Re-deem-er's
2 Je - sus! the name that charms our fears, That bids our sor-rows
3 He breaks the power of can - celed sin, He sets the pris -oner
4 He speaks, and, lis - ten-ing to His voice, New life the dead re -

praise, My great Re-deem-er's praise, The glo-ries of my God and
cease; That bids our sor-row's cease;'Tis mu-sic in the sin - ner's
free, He sets the pris-oner free; His blood can make the foul - est
ceive, New life the dead re - ceive, The mourn-ful bro - ken hearts re-

King. The tri - umphs of His grace. The
ears, 'Tis life, and health, and peace, 'Tis
clean, His blood a - vailed for me. His
joice, The hum - ble poor be - lieve. The

1 The tri - umphs of His grace, The tri - umphs of His

tri - umphs of His grace, The tri - umphs of His grace!
life, and health, and peace, 'Tis life, and health, and peace.
blood a - vailed for me, His blood a - vailed for me.
hum - ble poor be - lieve The hum - ble poor be - lieve.

grace, The tri - umphs of His grace, The tri-umphs of His grace!

5 Hear Him, ye deaf; His praise, ye dumb.
  // Your loosened tongues employ; //
  Ye blind, behold your Savior come;
  /// And leap, ye lame, for joy! ///

6 My gracious Master and my God,
  // Assist me to proclaim, //
  To spread through all the earth abroad
  /// The honors of Thy name. ///

82. Kum Ba Yah

Traditional African melody

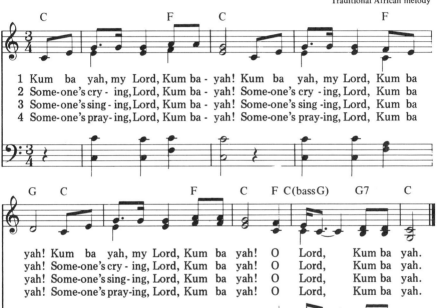

1 Kum ba yah, my Lord, Kum ba - yah! Kum ba yah, my Lord, Kum ba
2 Some-one's cry - ing, Lord, Kum ba - yah! Some-one's cry - ing, Lord, Kum ba
3 Some-one's sing - ing, Lord, Kum ba - yah! Some-one's sing - ing, Lord, Kum ba
4 Some-one's pray- ing, Lord, Kum ba - yah! Some-one's pray-ing, Lord, Kum ba

yah! Kum ba yah, my Lord, Kum ba yah! O Lord, Kum ba yah.
yah! Some-one's cry - ing, Lord, Kum ba yah! O Lord, Kum ba yah.
yah! Some-one's sing- ing, Lord, Kum ba yah! O Lord, Kum ba yah.
yah! Some-one's pray-ing, Lord, Kum ba yah! O Lord, Kum ba yah.

Additional stanzas:

/// In Your body, Lord, we are one. ///
O Lord, we are one.

/// In this banquet, Lord, we find strength. ///
O Lord, we find strength.

/// Draw us nearer, Lord, each to each. ///
O Lord, each to each.

/// Fill our mind, Lord, with Your peace. ///
O Lord, with Your peace.

/// Undivided, Lord, we shall stand. ///
O Lord, we shall stand.

83. O Lord of Every Shining Constellation

ANCIENT OF DAYS (Albany)

Albert F. Bayly (1901-)

J. Albert Jeffrey, 1886

1 O Lord of ev - ery shin - ing con - stel - la - tion
2 You, Lord, have made the at - om's hid - den forc - es,
3 O life, a - wak - ing life in cell and tis - sue,
4 You, Lord, have stamped Your im - age on Your crea - tures,

That wheels in splen - dor through the mid - night sky,
Your laws its might - y en - er - gies ful - fill;
From flower to bird, from beast to brain of man,
And though they mar that image, love them still; ___

Grant us Your Spir - it's true il - lum - in - a - tion
Teach us, to whom You give such rich re - sourc - es,
O help us trace, from birth to fi - nal is - sue,
Up - lift our eyes to Christ, that in His feat - ures

To read the sec - rets of Your work on high.
In all we use, to serve Your ho - ly will.
The sure un - fold - ing of Your age - less plan.
We may dis - cern the beau - ty of Your will.

84. O Sing, My Soul, Your Maker's Praise

Psalm 34
Original text (Finnish): Julius Krohn (1835-1888)
English translation: E.E. Ryden and Toivo Harjunpää, 1962

Finnish traditional melody
Harmony, O.S.

1 O sing, my soul, your Ma - ker's praise in grate - ful hymns as -
2 The Lord is good to those who seek His face in time of
3 The Lord will turn His face in peace when trou - bled souls draw

cend - ing, Whose stead - fast love has crowned thy days with heav - 'nly
sor - row: He giv - eth strength un - to the weak, and grace for
near Him; His lov - ing - kind - ness ne'er will cease to them that

gifts un - end - ing. I sought the Lord, He heard my cry; His
each to - mor - row. Though grief may tar - ry for the night, the
trust and fear Him. Our God will not for - sake His own, e -

ho - ly an - gels hov - er nigh the tents of those who love Him.
morn shall break in joy and light with bless - ings from His pres - ence.
ter - nal is His heav - 'nly throne; His king - dom stands for - ev - er.

85. Planted Wheat

HASHUAL
Traditional Hebrew melody
Arr. by Jeff Cothran

Jeff Cothran

Simply and lightly

Introduction

Recorder
and voices: **Noo Noo Noo, etc.**

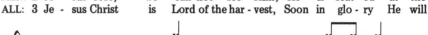

Verse

MEN: 1 Plan-ted wheat, with-in the wheat-fields, wait-ing till the sum-mer-
MEN: 2 Je-sus rose, we can-not see Him; He is seat-ed at the
ALL: 3 Je-sus Christ is Lord of the har-vest, Soon in glo-ry He will

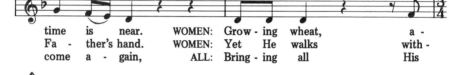

time is near. WOMEN: Grow-ing wheat, a-
Fa-ther's hand. WOMEN: Yet He walks with-
come a-gain, ALL: Bring-ing all His

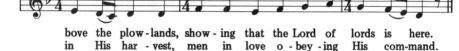

bove the plow-lands, show-ing that the Lord of lords is here.
in His har-vest, men in love o-bey-ing His com-mand.
ho-ly an-gels, gath-'ring in the ri-pened sheaves of grain.

Refrain

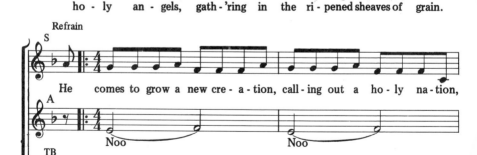

S

He comes to grow a new cre-a-tion, call-ing out a ho-ly na-tion,

A

Noo Noo

TB

He comes to grow a new cre-a-tion, call-ing out a ho-ly na-tion,

*Wood block, finger cymbals, or clapping.

all who will be-lieve, and all who will re-ceive. He

Noo Noo Noo Noo Noo Noo

all who will be-lieve, and all who will re-ceive. He

86. Lord, We Praise You

Otis Skillings

Otis Skillings

1 Lord, we praise You. Lord, we praise You,
2 Lord, we love You. Lord, we love You,
3 Al - le - lu - ia! Al - le - lu - ia!

Lord, we praise You. We praise You, Lord.
Lord, we love You. We love You, Lord.
Al - le - lu - ia! Al - le - lu - ia!

87. Praise and Thanksgiving

LOBET UND PREISET
Alsatian round

Paraphrase of the German

Praise and thanks - giv - ing let ev - 'ry - one bring Un - to the

Fa - ther for ev - 'ry good thing. All to - geth - er joy - ful - ly sing!

88. The Lord Hath Done Great Things

Noah Zuercher, stanza 1
Harold Thiessen, stanzas 2, 3, 4
Paraphrase of Psalms 3:2-4; 29:4, 5; 126:3, 5, 6; and Exodus 1:14

Harold Thiessen

1 The Lord hath done great things for us and
2 That voice of the Lord is more pow - er - ful than
3 He is my glo - ry who lifts my head, my
4 He that sows in tears shall reap in joy, go - ing

there - fore we re - joice. Our chains of bond-age
all the hosts that op - press. He breaks the ce - dars of
shield and strength to ful - fill. I cried to the Lord now
forth bear - ing pre - cious seeds. He shall sure - ly come with

melt a - way be - fore His might - y voice.
Leb - a - non, and shakes the wil - der - ness.
with my voice, as He spoke from His ho - ly hill.
strength a - gain and re - joic - ing bring-ing His sheaves. A-men, A - men.

89. O, Freedom

Negro spiritual   Traditional

O,_____ free - dom, O,_____ free - dom,
No more moan - ing, No more moan - ing,
There'll be sing - ing, There'll be sing - ing,
There'll be shout - ing, There'll be shout - ing,
There'll be pray - ing, There'll be pray - ing,
O,_____ free - dom, O,_____ free - dom

O,_____ free - dom o - ver me.
No more moan - ing o - ver me.
There'll be sing - ing o - ver me.
There'll be shout - ing o - ver me.
There'll be pray - ing o - ver me.
O,_____ free - dom o - ver me.

And be - fore I'd be a slave I'll be

bur - ied in my grave And go

home To my Lord and be free.

90. Peace Like a River

Traditional

Spiritual

91. Praise the Lord

Majestic

I can

hear His mu-sic in my soul.
bone, ev'ry mus-cle in my frame, Praise the Lord! Praise the
fishes join in the might-y choir,

And it sings in my heart like a hot and blaz-ing coal.
Lord! { And re-joice in His high and ho-ly name. Praise the
Light my song with Your high and ho-ly fire.

Lord! Praise the Lord!

Through the day, through the night, in the
Praise with tongue, nose and eye, while I
Each con-di-tion of man-kind, shares the

dark-ness in the light, each con - di - tion of my life comes from His
live, when I die. Ev - 'ry at - om of my be - ing, sing His
cho - rus, give the sign. Prais - ing God is the priv - i - lege of

hand: In the clouds, un - der-ground, on the sea, on the land,⎫
praise: Praise His love, praise His hate, praise His thoughts, praise His ways⎬ Praise the
all: Black and white, straight and gay, old and young, short and tall,⎭

Lord! Praise the Lord! Praise the Lord!

2 Ev - 'ry
3 Rocks and

Lord!

92. Praise for Bread

From NORFOLK CHIMES
Arr. by Clarence Dickinson

Albert R. Ledoux, alt.

Morn - ing
Noon - time has come, the board is spread;
Even - ing

thanks be to God, who gives us bread;* Praise God for bread!*

*Additional stanzas: "work," "rest."

93. Praise the Lord! Praise, O Servants

Psalm 113:1-2
Additional stanzas by Marjorie Jillson, 1971

Heinz Werner Zimmermann, 1970

1 Praise the Lord! Praise, O ser - vants of the Lord,
2 Praise the Lord! Thanks and prais - es sing to God,
3 Praise the Lord! Praise and glo - ry give to God!
4 Praise the Lord! Praise, you ser - vants of the Lord!

praise the name of the Lord! Bless - ed be the name of the Lord!
day by day to the Lord! High a - bove the na - tions is God,
Who is like un - to Him? Rais - ing up the poor from the dust,
Praise the love of the Lord! Giv - ing to the home-less a home,

Bless - ed be the name of the Lord from this time forth and for-
high a - bove the na - tions is God. His glo - ry high o - ver
Rais - ing up the poor from the dust, He makes them dwell in His
Giv - ing to the home-less a home, He fills their hearts with new

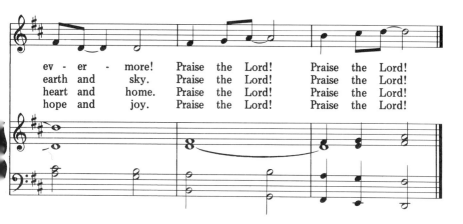

ev - er - more!	Praise	the	Lord!	Praise	the	Lord!
earth and sky.	Praise	the	Lord!	Praise	the	Lord!
heart and home.	Praise	the	Lord!	Praise	the	Lord!
hope and joy.	Praise	the	Lord!	Praise	the	Lord!

94. Spirit of the Living God

Daniel Iverson, 1926   Daniel Iverson, 1926

Spir - it of the liv - ing God, Now de-scend on me! Spir - it of the

liv - ing God, Now de-scend on me! Break me, melt me, Mold me,

fill me! Spir - it of the liv - ing God, Now de-scend on me! A - men.

95. Prayer of St. Francis

Francis of Assisi

Sebastian Temple
Arr. by Lavern Wagner

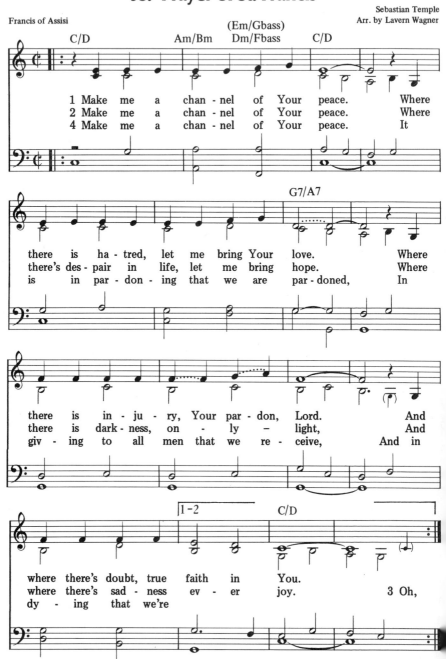

96. Rise and Shine

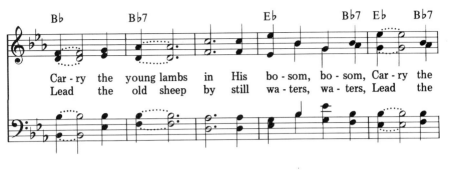

Car - ry the young lambs in His bo - som, bo - som, Car - ry the
Lead the old sheep by still wa - ters, wa - ters, Lead the

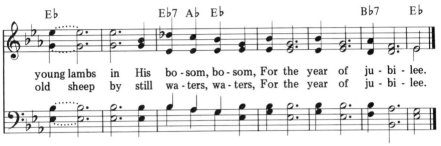

young lambs in His bo - som, bo - som, For the year of ju - bi - lee.
old sheep by still wa - ters, wa - ters, For the year of ju - bi - lee.

2 Oh,—come on,—mourners, get you ready, ready,
   Come on,—mourners, get you ready, ready, *(Repeat)*
      For the year of jubilee;
   You may keep—your lamps—trimmed and burning, burning,
   Keep—your lamps—trimmed and burning, burning, *(Repeat)*
      For the year of jubilee.
        Refrain: Oh, rise and shine, etc.

3 Oh,—come on,—children, don't be weary, weary,
   Come on,— children, don't be weary, weary, *(Repeat)*
      For the year of jubilee.
   Oh,—don't—you hear them bells a-ringing, ringing,
   Don't—you hear them bells a-ringing, ringing, *(Repeat)*
      For the year of jubilee.
        Refrain: Oh, rise and shine, etc.

97. Sermon on the Mount

Matthew 5:3-11
Paul Quinlan

Paul Quinlan
Accomp., O.S.

Stanzas

1 Bless-ed are the poor in spir-it; Bless-ed are the poor in spir-it; Bless-ed are the poor in spir-it; theirs is the king-dom of God.

2 Bless-ed is the man who is hum-ble; Bless-ed is the man who is hum-ble; Bless-ed is the man who is hum-ble; he'll win pos-ses-sion of the land.

3 Bless-ed are the ones now in mourn-ing; Bless-ed are the ones now in mourn-ing; Bless-ed are the ones now in mourn-ing; they'll have their com-fort one day.

4 Bless-ed all who thirst for jus-tice; Bless-ed all who thirst for jus-tice; Bless-ed all who thirst for jus-tice; for they will soon be sat-is-fied.

Refrain

On that moun-tain, Je-sus talk-ing with us;

on that moun - tain, Je - sus walk - ing with us;

on that moun - tain, Al - le - lu - ia! Al - le,-

Al - le - lu - ia! Sing out, all you chil - dren of the Lord.

5 Blessed is the man — of mercy; (3 times)
   he will have mercy in his turn.

6 Blessed are the clean — of heart; (3 times)
   they'll see the face — of the Lord.

7 Blessed are the peace — makers; (3 times)
   they are the children of their God.

8 Blessed are the sons — of justice; (3 times)
   theirs is the kingdom of the Lord.

98. Seek Ye First

Matthew 6:33

Karen Lafferty

99. Set My Spirit Free

Anonymous

Set my Spir-it free that I might wor-ship Thee, Set my Spir-it

free that I might praise Thy name, Let all bond-age go and let de-

liv-'rance flow, Set my Spir-it free to wor-ship Thee.

100. Son of the Father

Fred Kaan, 1972

Melody from Sri Lanka
Harmony, O.S.

1 Son of the Fa - ther, Je - sus, Lord and Slave,
2 Son of the Fa - ther, work - er's Friend,
3 Son of the Fa - ther, Auth - or of our faith,
4 Seed of the Fa - ther, from life's fur - row born,
5 Fa - ther and Spir - it, Je - sus, Lord and Man,

born a - mong the cat - tle in the squal - or of a cave,
You whom Jo - seph taught the skills of work - ing with Your hands,
choos - ing men to fol - low You from ev - 'ry walk of life,
teach - ing men in par - a - bles from ag - ri - cul - ture drawn,
bless us in the work You have ap - point - ed to be done.

one with God You made Your - self one with man, shun - ning wealth;
Man, at home in build - er's yard, one with man, toil - ing hard;
who with them, in boats on shore, trou - bles shared, bur - dens bore;
Je - sus, Lov - er of the soil, Man of earth, Son of toil;
Lift our spir - its, guide our wills, steer our hands, use our skills;

Lord, we wor - ship You with hand and mind.

Words copyrighted by Fred Kaan. Reprinted by permission.

101. Song of Good News

W.F. Jabusch

Traditional Israeli folk song

1 O - pen your ears, O Chris - tian peo - ple, O - pen your
2 He who has ears to hear His mes - sage, He who has
3 Is - ra - el comes to greet the Sav - ior; Ju - dah is

ears and hear good news! O - pen your hearts, O
ears, then let him hear! He who would learn the
glad to see His day! From East and West the

roy - al priest - hood, God has come to you.
way of wis - dom, let him hear God's Word.
peo - ples tra - vel, He will show the way.

Refrain:

God has spo - ken to His peo - ple, hal - le - lu - jah!

And His words are words of wis - dom, hal - le - lu - jah.

Suggestions for singing: Sing the stanzas quite slowly, then sing the refrain much more rapidly, feeling the rhythm as one beat to the measure. The last refrain may be repeated as often as desired, possibly singing each repeat a bit faster than the one before. Percussion instruments can be used for the refrain.

102. Teach Me Kingdom Ways

Nancy Miner, 1975

Nancy Miner, 1975

Refrain

Teach me king - dom ways so that I may walk with Thee,

Teach me king - dom ways so that I may walk with Thee,

Teach me king - dom ways so that I may walk with Thee,

till I stand be - fore Your throne, pre - cious Lord, glo - ry,

glo - ry, till I stand be - fore Your throne, pre - cious Lord. *Fine.*

Stanzas:

1 In a world of chains, teach me how to be free,
2 In a world of sin, teach me how to be pure,

In a world of masks, teach me how to be me.
In a world of doubts, teach me how to be sure.

Let me walk in peace in a world where there is none.
Let me walk in pow'r in a world that is weak.

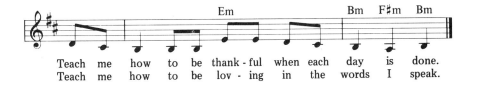

Teach me how to be thank - ful when each day is done.
Teach me how to be lov - ing in the words I speak.

103. Celebration Song

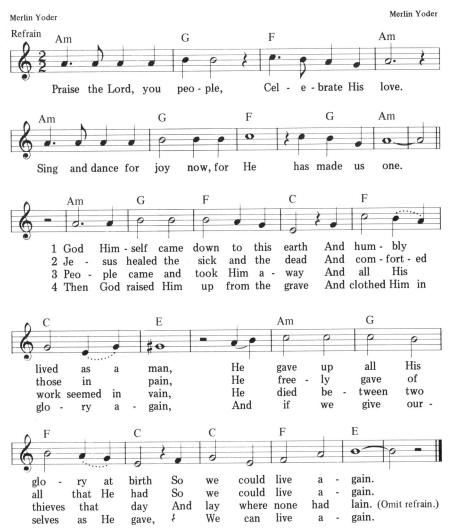

Merlin Yoder

Refrain

Praise the Lord, you peo - ple, Cel - e - brate His love.

Sing and dance for joy now, for He has made us one.

1 God Him - self came down to this earth And hum - bly
2 Je - sus healed the sick and the dead And com - fort - ed
3 Peo - ple came and took Him a - way And all His
4 Then God raised Him up from the grave And clothed Him in

lived as a man, He gave up all His
those in pain, He free - ly gave of
work seemed in vain, He died be - tween two
glo - ry a - gain, And if we give our -

glo - ry at birth So we could live a - gain.
all that He had So we could live a - gain.
thieves that day And lay where none had lain. (Omit refrain.)
selves as He gave, We can live a - gain.

Copyright © 1971 by Merlin Yoder. Used by permission.

104. Thanks Be to God

Original text: German
French by Joseph Gelineau

Herman Stern, 1943

Thanks be to God and all praise to His name!
Dan - ket dem Herrn und lob - singt sei - nem Na - men!
Gloire au Sei - gneur! et que vien - ne - son Rè - gne.

Reprinted from *Cantate Domino*, published by Baerenreiter - Verlag, Kassel, West Germany.

105. The Lord is Risen

C.P. Mudd

C.P. Mudd

Melody

C   D   G

1 The Lord   is ris - en to life,____
2 The Lord   will watch o - ver you,____
3 "My friends,   I   have a gift for you,____
4 "My friends,   look in each oth - er's eyes,____

The Lord is ris - en to life,____
The Lord will watch o - ver you,____
"My friends, I have a gift for you,____
"My friends, look in each oth - er's eyes,____

C   D   G

____ The Lord   is ris - en to life;____
____ The Lord   will smile when you laugh;____
____ A gift   that each of you must share,____
____ And if   my gift is - n't there____

The Lord is ris - en to life;____
The Lord will smile when you laugh;____
A gift   that each of you must share,____
And if   my gift is - n't there____

Copyright © 1970 by World Library Publications.

The Lord has con - quered sin and
The Lord will care in your mo - ment's
And share it well with the world a -
Then go and en - ter that lone - li -

(bass)
The Lord has con - quered sin and
The Lord will care in your mo - ment's
And share it well with the world a -
Then go and en - ter that lone - li -

death, and brought us back to life.
loss, and bring you back to life."
bout; the gift: it is my life."
ness, and give to all my life."

(bass)
death, and brought us back to life.
loss, and bring you back to life."
bout; the gift: it is my life."
ness, and give to all my life."

106. The True and Joyful Sun

Georg Weissel (1590-1635)
Original text: German
Tr. O.S., 1978

Melody based on MACHT HOCH DIE TÜR

The true and joy - ful Sun — is He, Who
Er ist die rech - te Freu - den - sonn, bringt

comes with loud ex - ul - tant glee: All praise be to my God!
mit sich lau - ter Freud und Wonn: ge - lo - bet sei mein Gott!

107. The Church Within Us

Kent Schneider
Alt. by Don Hustad

Kent Schneider

With strength

1 There's a church with - in us, O Lord; There's a
2 There's po - ten - tial with - in us, O Lord; Some - thing
3 There's a fire with - in us, O Lord; A new
4 There's a church with - in us, O Lord; There's some

church with - in us, O Lord; Not a build - ing, but a
stir - ring with - in us, O Lord; Some - thing strain - ing to have
life a - burn - ing, O Lord; A new fire for a
build - ing to be done,— O Lord; Not with steel, not with

soul, Not a por - tion, but a whole; There's a
birth, To be vis - i - ble on earth, There's po -
life, Com - bat - ting pres - ent strife, There's a
stone, But with lives which are Your own, There's a

*optional chord

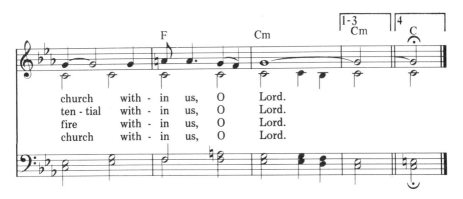

church with - in us, O Lord.
ten - tial with - in us, O Lord.
fire with - in us, O Lord.
church with - in us, O Lord.

108. Shalom Chaverim

Original text: Hebrew
English by A.D.Z.

From *101 Rounds*

Sha - lom, my friends! Sha - lom, my friends! Sha - lom, Sha - lom!
Sha - lom cha - ve - rim! Sha - lom, cha - ve - rim! Sha - lom, Sha - lom!
Fare - well, good friends! Fare - well, good friends! Fare-well, Fare - well!

We'll see you a - gain, we'll see you a - gain, Sha - lom, Sha - lom!
Le - hit - ra - ot, le - hit - ra - ot, Sha - lom, Sha - lom!
Till we meet a - gain, till we meet a - gain, Fare - well, Fare-well!

Copyright ©1959 by Cooperative Recreation Service, from *Chansons de Notre Chalet*.
Used by permission of World Around Songs.

109. Sing and Rejoice

W. H. Bradbury

Sing and re - joice; Sing and re - joice;
Ho - san - na! Ho - san - na!

Let all things liv - ing now sing and re - joice.
And on earth peace to all men of good will!

From *Sacred Canons*. Used by permission of World Around Songs.

110. The Foot-Washing Song

Adapted from John 13

Shirley Lewis Brown
Arr. by R.J. Batastini

Gracefully

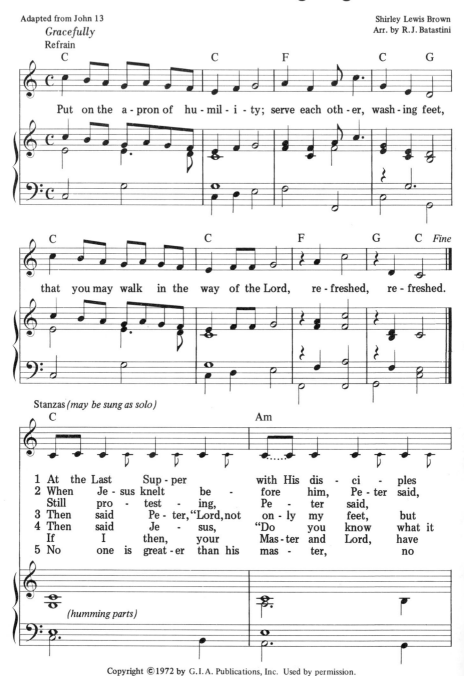

Refrain

Put on the a-pron of hu-mil-i-ty; serve each oth-er, wash-ing feet,

that you may walk in the way of the Lord, re-freshed, re-freshed. *Fine*

Stanzas *(may be sung as solo)*

1 At the Last Sup-per with His dis-ci-ples
2 When Je-sus knelt be-fore him, Pe-ter said,
  Still pro-test-ing, Pe-ter said,
3 Then said Pe-ter, "Lord, not on-ly my feet, but
4 Then said Je-sus, "Do you know what it
  If I then, your Mas-ter and Lord, have
5 No one is great-er than his mas-ter, no

(humming parts)

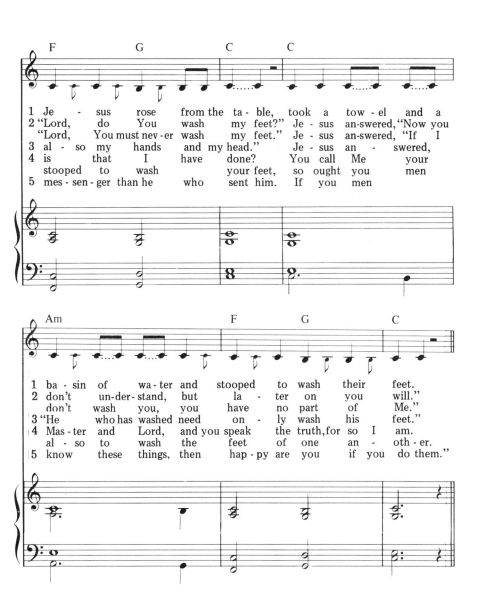

111. Take the Dark Strength of Our Nights

Jamaican folk song
Arr. Doreen Potter, 1972
Accomp., O.S.

John Hoad, 1971

1 Take the dark strength of our nights, soft with pee - ny
2 Take the pro - test of our need, what the gar - den?
3 Take the is - land's hu - man skills, danc - ing seas and

wal - lies'* lights. Take the star - signs wheel - ing round,
what the weed? Take the orb___ and break the chain,
wise old hills. Take our Je - sus and His power,

while the steel - drum melts to sound. Take and weave a
break the shack - les of the brain. Take and weave a
match His peo - ple to this hour. Take and weave a

womb of night that we may live, that we may live.
womb of right that we may live, that we may live.
womb of light that we may live, that we may live.

*"Peeney wallies" is a Jamaican term for "fireflies."

Reprinted from *Cantate Domino*, published by Baerenreiter-Verlag, Kassel, West Germany.

112. The Jesus Road
(Jesus Hemeo?o Eno?ke Pavaetse)

Original text: Cheyenne

Cheyenne spiritual song

The Je - sus, the Je - sus road. This road a - lone is true.

This true road a - lone is fill'd with good-ness. Ac - cept this road of

Je - sus. Re -joice in Him and for this way be glad each day.

On this road the Ho - ly Spir - it guides you.

Jesus hemeo?o eno?ke - pavaetse.
Jesus' road alone is good.

Eno?ke - one?seomotse. Vena - hestanomova.
It alone is true. Accept it!

Ve?še - hetotaetanoo oešeeva.
Rejoice because of it every day.

Ma?heone - mahta?sooma néstse - ameotséhaevo.
The Holy Spirit will lead you.

Cheyenne songs are sung in unison without instrumental accompaniment. Normally they are repeated two or three times. This arrangement has been made with non - Cheyenne singers in mind. The original melody has been preserved as accurately as the English text permits. The suggested accompaniment is a simple, percussive rhythm, based on the pentatonic (5 - note) structure of the melody.

Original Cheyenne text transcribed and translated literally by Malcolm Wenger. Adapted by O. S. from the singing of Lyle and Evelyn Redbird and Bertha Whiteman as recorded by Malcolm Wenger, May, 1976.

113. The Joy of the Lord

Alliene G. Vale

Alliene G. Vale

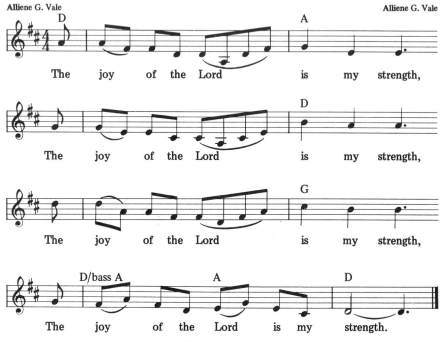

The joy of the Lord is my strength,

The joy of the Lord is my strength,

The joy of the Lord is my strength,

The joy of the Lord is my strength.

"Peace" or "Spirit" can be substituted for "joy." Further stanzas can be added.

114. There's a Wideness in God's Mercy

GOTT WILL'S MACHEN
J.L. Steiner
Arr., O.S.

Frederick William Faber, 1862

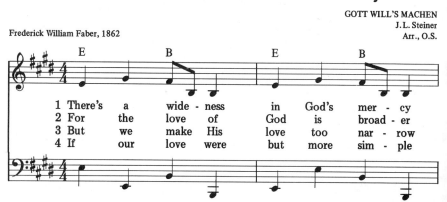

1 There's a wide - ness in God's mer - cy
2 For the love of God is broad - er
3 But we make His love too nar - row
4 If our love were but more sim - ple

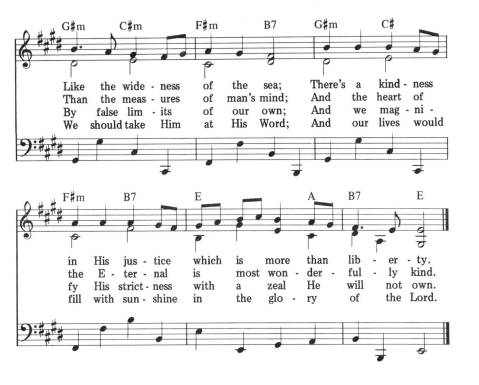

G#m C#m F#m B7 G#m C#

Like the wide - ness of the sea; There's a kind - ness
Than the meas - ures of man's mind; And the heart of
By false lim - its of our own; And we mag - ni -
We should take Him at His Word; And our lives would

F#m B7 E A B7 E

in His jus - tice which is more than lib - er - ty.
the E - ter - nal is most won - der - ful - ly kind.
fy His strict - ness with a zeal He will not own.
fill with sun - shine in the glo - ry of the Lord.

115. Christ Is Arisen

Original text: German, 1529   Anon. 1964

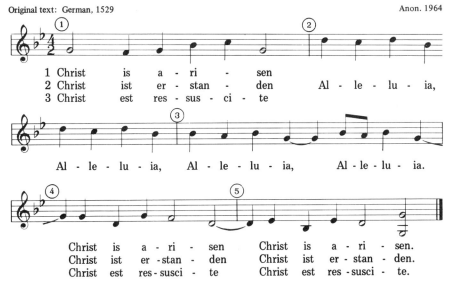

1 Christ is a - ri - sen
2 Christ ist er - stan - den Al - le - lu - ia,
3 Christ est res - sus - ci - te

Al - le - lu - ia, Al - le - lu - ia, Al - le - lu - ia.

Christ is a - ri - sen   Christ is a - ri - sen.
Christ ist er - stan - den   Christ ist er - stan - den.
Christ est res - susci - te   Christ est res - susci - te.

From *Cantate Domino*. Used by permission of Baerenreiter-Verlag.

116. The Spirit of the Lord

Luke 4:18, 19

Esther Wiebe

1 The Spir - it of the Lord is up - on me, The Spir - it of the Lord is up - on me, He has a -

Note: This arrangement was originally intended for choirs but can be sung by congregations. Suggestions for singing portions only by men or women need not be followed but are appropriate.

Used by permission from *Fill My House, Compositions and Arrangements for Church Choirs* by Esther Wiebe, copyright and published by Canadian Mennonite Bible College, Winnipeg, Manitoba, 1975.

noin - ted me to preach the good news, to

preach the good news to the poor. The

Women and Men

Spir - it of the Lord is up - on me, The

Spir - it of the Lord is up - on me.

Spir - it of the Lord, come up - on me; O

Spir - it of the Lord, come up - on me.

117. The Strife Is O'er

Anonymous, Köln, 1695
Trans., Francis Pott

James Minchin

Introduction only

1 The strife is o'er, the
2 The powers of death have
3 The three sad days have

Octaves

bat - tle done;   Now is the Vic - tor's tri - umph won;
done their worst;   But Je - sus has His foes dis - persed;
quick - ly sped   He ri - ses glo - rious from the dead;

O let the song of praise be sung:
Let shouts of praise and joy out - burst:
All glo - ry to our ri - sen Head:

Refrain

Al - le - lu - ia!   Al - le - lu - ia!

Al - le - lu - ia!   Al - le - lu - ia!   Al - le - lu - ia!   Al - le - lu - ia!

Al - le - lu - ia! Praise the Lord!

118. This Is the Day, This Is the Day

Fiji Islands
Folk melody

Anonymous

1 This is the day, this is the day that the
2 Come un - to Me, come un - to Me, oh My
3 Sing and be glad, sing and be glad, for the

Lord has made that the Lord has made. Let us re - joice,
peo - ple come, oh My peo - ple come. Sing praise to Him,
Lord is good, for the Lord is good. He's done great things,

let us re - joice and be glad in it, and be glad in it.
Sing praise to Him, I will make you one, I will make you one.
He's done great things as He said He would, as He said He would.

1 This is the day that the Lord has made.
  Let us re - joice and be glad in it.
2 Come un - to Me, oh, My peo - ple come.
  Sing praise to Him, I will make you one.
3 Sing and be glad for the Lord is good.
  He's done great things as He said He would.

This is the day, this is the day that the Lord has made.

119. The Virgin Mary Had a Baby Boy

West Indian traditional carol

West Indian traditional carol
Collected, Edric Connor
Arr. by Elizabeth Poston

Bright and joyful

1. The Vir - gin Ma - ry had a Ba - by Boy,[1] The Vir - gin Ma - ry had a Ba - by Boy, The Vir - gin Ma - ry had a Ba - by Boy,
2. The an - gels sang when the Ba - by born,[2] The an - gels sang when the Ba - by born, The an - gels sang when the Ba - by born,
3. The wise men saw when the Ba - by born, The wise men saw where the Ba - by born, The wise men went where the Ba - by born,

And they say that His name was Je - sus.

[1] In the original "De Virgin Mary."

[2] In the original "De Baby born."

Taken down from the singing of the Negro James Bryce in 1942 when Bryce was 92 years old.

Reprinted by permission from *The Cambridge Hymnal*, 1967, Cambridge University Press, London, England.

120. There in God's Garden

Pécselyi Kiràly Imre 1961 körül
Trans., Erik Routley, 1973
German: Dieter Trautwein and Vilmos Gyöngyösi

Hungarian melody, 1744
Harmony, O.S.

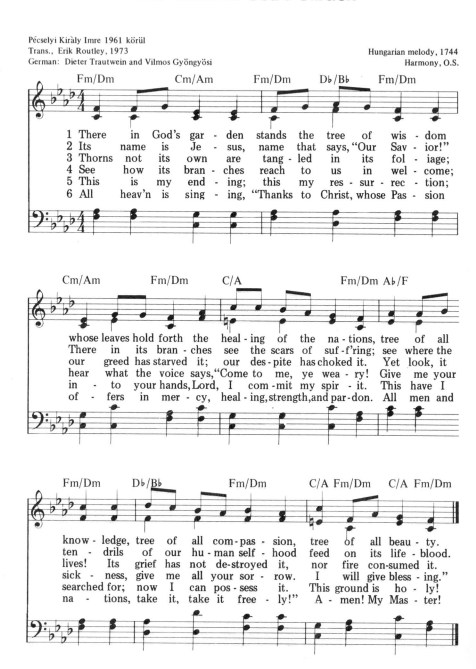

1 There in God's gar - den stands the tree of wis - dom
2 Its name is Je - sus, name that says, "Our Sav - ior!"
3 Thorns not its own are tang - led in its fol - iage;
4 See how its bran - ches reach to us in wel - come;
5 This is my end - ing; this my res - ur - rec - tion;
6 All heav'n is sing - ing, "Thanks to Christ, whose Pas - sion

whose leaves hold forth the heal - ing of the na - tions, tree of all
There in its bran - ches see the scars of suf - f'ring; see where the
our greed has starved it; our des - pite has choked it. Yet look, it
hear what the voice says, "Come to me, ye wea - ry! Give me your
in - to your hands, Lord, I com - mit my spir - it. This have I
of - fers in mer - cy, heal - ing, strength, and par - don. All men and

know - ledge, tree of all com - pas - sion, tree of all beau - ty.
ten - drils of our hu - man self - hood feed on its life - blood.
lives! Its grief has not de - stroyed it, nor fire con - sumed it.
sick - ness, give me all your sor - row. I will give bless - ing."
searched for; now I can pos - sess it. This ground is ho - ly!
na - tions, take it, take it free - ly!" A - men! My Mas - ter!

German:

1 Du schöner Lebensbaum des Paradieses,
　gütiger Jesus, Gottes Lamm auf Erden.
　Du bist der wahre Retter unsres Lebens,
　unser Befreier.

2 Nur unsretwegen hattest du zu leiden,
　gingst an das Kreuz und trugst die Dornenkrone.
　Für unsre Sünden musstest du bezahlen
　mit deinem Leben.

3 Lieber Herr Jesus, wandle uns von Grund auf,
　dass allen denen wir auch gern vergeben,
　die uns beleidigt, die uns Unrecht taten,
　selbst sich verfehlten.

4 Für diese alle wollen wir dich bitten,
　nach deinem Vorbild laut zum Vater flehen,
　dass wir mit vielen Heilgen zu dir kommen
　in deinen Frieden.

5 Wenn sich die Tage unsres Lebens neigen,
　nimm unsren Geist, Herr, auf in deine Hände,
　dass wir zuletzt von hier getröstet scheiden,
　Lob auf den Lippen.

6 Dank sei dem Vater, unsrem Gott im Himmel,
　er ist der Retter der verlornen Menschheit,
　hat uns erworben Frieden ohne Ende,
　ewige Freude.

121. Stay with Us, Savior

Original text: German
French by Joseph Gelineau

Albert Thate

Stay with us, Sav - ior, for ev' - ning is
Herr, blei - be bei - uns, denn es will A - bend
Sei - gneur, reste a - vec nous, dé - jà le jour dé -

com - ing and to - mor - row is an - oth - er day.
wer - den, und der Tag hat sich ge - nei - get.
cli - ne et la nuit est tou - te pro - che.

122. The King of Glory

W. F. Jabusch

Traditional Israeli folk song

The King of glo - ry comes, the na - tion re - joic - es.

O - pen the gates be - fore Him, lift up your voic - es.

1 Who is the King of glo - ry; how shall we call Him?
2 In all of Gal - i - lee, in cit - y or vil - lage,
3 Sing then of Dav - id's Son, our Sav - ior and Bro - ther;
4 He gave His life for us, the pledge of sal - va - tion,
5 He con - quered sin and death; He tru - ly has ris - en.

He is Em - man - u - el, the prom - ised of a - ges.
He goes a - mong His peo - ple cur - ing their ill - ness.
In all of Gal - i - lee was nev - er an - oth - er.
He took up - on Him - self the sins of the na - tion.
And He will share with us His heav - en - ly vi - sion.

Copyright © 1967 by Willard F. Jabusch, St. Mary of the Lake Seminary, Mundelein, IL 60060.

123. Sing and Rejoice in the Lord

Original text: German

Hermann Stern

Sing_____ and re - joice_____ in the Lord in your
Sin - get und spie - let dem Herrn_____ in

hearts with thanks - giv - ing, sing_____ and re - joice in Him.
eu - ren_____ Her - zen, sin - get und spie - let.

Reprinted from *Cantate Domino*, published by Baerenreiter - Verlag, Kassel, West Germany.

124. There Is a Balm in Gilead

Negro spiritual
Arr. by J. Harold Moyer
Alt. by O.S.

Negro spiritual

There is a balm in Gil-e-ad To make the wound-ed whole.

There is a balm in Gil-e-ad To heal the sin-sick soul.

1 Some-times I feel dis-cour-aged, And think my works in vain,—
2 Don't ev-er feel dis-cour-aged, For Je-sus is your Friend
3 If you can-not preach like Pe-ter, If you can-not pray like Paul,—

But then the Ho-ly Spir-it, Re-vives my soul a-gain.
And if you lack for know-ledge, He'll not re-fuse to lend.
You can tell the love of Je-sus And say, "He died for all."

Note: Stanzas may be sung by sopranos only or by a solo voice while others hum their parts.

125. This Is the Day That the Lord Has Made

Cyril A. Reilly
Harmony, Roger Nachtwey
Accomp., O.S.

Cyril A. Reilly

1 This is the day that the Lord has made.
2 This is the day when the Lord a - rose.
3 This is the day when we rise with Him. Let us be glad
4 This is the day all the world is new.

and re - joice in it! Let us be glad and re - joice!

Refrain:

This is the day that the Lord has made.
This is the day when the Lord a - rose!
This is the day when we rise with Him! Al - le - lu - ia,
This is the day all the world is new!

Al - le - lu - ia! Al - le - lu - ia is our song of joy!

Sing the song we will sing for - ev - er: Al - le - lu - ia,

al - le - lu - ia! Al - le - lu - ia, al - le - lu - ia!

126. The Lord Be Praised

Julie Camp   Julie Camp

1 The Lord be praised, let the Lord be praised, In Him I
2 The Lord be praised, let the Lord be praised, From Him all

trust, I am not a - fraid. He is my strength, He
bless - ings free - ly flow. He com - forts, heals, He

is my song. The Lord be praised, praise His ho - ly name.
saves, He calms. The Lord be praised, praise His ho - ly name.

127. Travel On

Sydney Carter

Sydney Carter

Refrain

Gm

1 Trav - el on, trav - el
2 Trav - el on, trav - el
3 Trav - el on, trav - el
4 Trav - el on, trav - el

F   Dm   Cm/Gm

on, there's a riv - er that is flow - ing, A riv - er that is
on, there's a flow-er that is grow - ing, A flow - er that is
on, to the mu - sic that is play - ing, The mu - sic that is
on, to the king-dom that is com - ing The king-dom that is

Dm   Gm   B♭

flow - ing night and day.   Trav - el on, trav - el
grow - ing night and day.   Trav - el on, trav - el
play - ing night and day.   Trav - el on, trav - el
com - ing night and day.   Trav - el on, trav - el

128. 'Tis the Gift to Be Simple

Stanza 1, Traditional
Stanza 2, Ron Klug

Shaker hymn tune

'Tis the gift to be sim - ple, 'Tis the gift to be free,
'Tis the gift to come down where we ought to be,
And when we find our - selves in the place just right,
'Twill be in the val - ley of love and de - light.

Love is the gift of God a - bove. He comes to us
Come then and go a - long with me. We'll go to the

all with His gifts of love, And we will be His
new land where we will be free, And we will live in

peo - ple if we heed His call And we'll
har - mo - ny and peace once a - gain And we'll

live in peace and with love to all.
share the love of God to all men.

129. Unity

Based on Philippians 2:1-8
Gerald Derstine

Gerald Derstine
Accomp., O.S.

130. Water of Life

New words and adaptation of
John 4:7-26 by John Ylvisaker

Traditional music
Arr. by John Ylvisaker

1 A_____ wom - an of Sa - mar - ia came to where the
2 _____ "If you knew who speaks to you a_____
3 The Sa - mar - i - tan wom - an want - ed this__
4 _____ Fin - al - ly Je - sus told_____ her ev - 'ry-
5 She_____ drop - ped her jar and ve - ry quick - ly_____

well of Ja - cob lies. Je sus____ said, "Give
Man, who is a Jew, you'd ask Him__ for the
wa ter, don't you see? But Je - sus____ ask - ed her,
thing that she had done. And the Sa - mar - i - tan
ran to tell the town. You know that__ man - y Sa -

Me a drink!" and the wom - an was sur - prised!
wa - ter of life, and He'd give it un - to you."
"Won't you please bring your hus - band un - to Me?"
wom - an knew that the Pro - phet now had come.
mar - i - tans be - lieved what she had found.

He who drinks of the wa - ter of life,
He who drinks of the wa - ter of life will nev - er thirst a - gain.

He will nev - er thirst a - gain.
He who drinks of the wa - ter of life will nev - er thirst a - gain.

This is a very simple, repetitive tune which should invite lots of improvisation and harmonization. One way to sing the song is to have a leader sing the first line and have the audience sing it back with harmony. It's called "lining out" the tune, a style of singing we seldom use, since we always seem to have printed lyrics in front of us.

131. We Thank Thee, Lord, for This Our Food

(The Blessing Song)

Anon.

Traditional

We thank Thee, Lord, for this our food; God is love,____ God is love.____ But more be-cause of Je - sus' blood; God is love,____ God is love. These mer - cies bless, and grant that we may eat and drink, and live with Thee, May eat and drink and live with Thee; God is love,____ God is love.____ A - men.

Handed down in Roy Roth family. Transcribed by Mrs. Roth and arranged by Floyd Brunk
(Family Music Camp, 1963). Courtesy Roy Roth.

132. We Who Bear the Human Name

Masao Takenaka and
Fred Kaan, 1972
German: Dieter Trautwein, 1973

Nj. R. Sutisno

We who bear the hu-man name are like flow-ers of the field;
E - ven Sol - o - mon of old, (said our Lord the Man of peace)
We are peo-ple of the field, crowd-ing A - sia's cit - y streets.

with-out sta - tus, with-out fame, tram-pled down and made to yield.
with his glo - ry and his gold could not match the flow-ers' grace.
We are peo-ple called to build a com-mun - i - ty of peace.

Un - pro - tect - ed and ex - posed to the scorch-ing wind that blows.
We are weak, but we re - call how the might - y men must fall.
We re - mem-ber as we toil hope is spring-ing from the soil.

Let all the world now blos - som as a field.

German:

1 Wer den Menschennamen trägt, gleicht den Blumen auf dem feld:
   ohne Geltung, ohne Rang, oft zertreten, hingemäht,
   Ungeschützt und ausgesetzt einem Wind, der alles dörrt.
   Lasst doch die Welt jetzt blühen wie ein Feld!

2 Auch ein Mann wie Salomo, sagte Jesus unser Herr,
   übertraf mit Ruhm und Gold nicht der Blumen Herrlichkeit.
   Wir sind schwach, doch uns ist klar: Wer der Macht vertraut, verliert.
   Lasst doch die Welt jetzt blühen wie ein Feld!

3 Wir sind Volk von diesem Feld, Asiens Städte füllen wir.
   Wir sind Volk, das bauen soll eine Welt, die Frieden kennt.
   Wir erfahr'n wenn wir uns müh'n wie die Hoffnung um uns wächst.
   Lasst doch die Welt jetzt blühen wie ein Feld!

133. Well, It's a New Day

J. H. Miffleton

J. H. Miffleton

Refrain

Em ... D

Well, it's a new day, Think new thoughts, for there's a new

Em ... C ... D ... *(Fine)* Em

way, Change your hearts, there's a new law in the land.

Stanzas

Em ... Am

1 A man can kill with a knife of steel, with a
2 An eye for an eye, and a tooth for a tooth,
3 You shall love the Lord your God, and your

C7maj. ... B7 ... Em

gun, a bomb or a lance ⎞
That was the law of the land. ⎬ 1-3 But there's a new law,
neigh bor as your - selves ⎠

D ... C ... D ... *Repeat Refrain* Em

there's a new law ⎧ A man can kill with a glance.
⎨ ⁊ Love makes a great-er de-mand.
⎩ ⁊ Love your en-e-my as well.

134. What Will I Do?

The Bawbees*

MASSON
The Bawbees

1 My Lord, my Lord, when I think of the wrongs
2 There are those who starve while I eat my fill,
3 There are those who suf - fer for the col - or of their skin,
4 Je sus lived and died you and me to save,
5 I must love my neigh - bor, my fel - low - man,

In this world I feel so blue; My Lord,
Lord, it makes me feel so blue; They hun - ger
Lord, it makes me feel so blue; 'Cause I'm sure
Lord, it makes me feel so blue; Did He go
Then I won't feel so blue; And help those

my Lord, won't You tell me please, Tell me
and thirst, get no help when they're ill; Tell me
we're all the same with - in; Tell me
in vain to a bor - rowed grave? Tell me
in need as best I can, That's what

what do You want me to do. (What will I do?)
what do You want me to do. (What will I do?)
what do You want me to do. (What will I do?)
what do You want me to do. (What will I do?)
my Lord wants me to do. (That's what I'll do.)

*A reflection on the injustices of present - day society.

From *Sing*, by the Department of Education of the Church of Scotland; used by permission of Ronald Beasley.

135. When He Comes Back

Malcolm Stewart

Malcolm Stewart

Refrain

When He comes back, when He comes back, Our lamps will be
burn-ing to wel-come Him when He comes back. *Fine*

Stanzas

1 The Mas-ter has pro-mised that He will re-turn On a
2 Look not for the Mas-ter in hea-ven's dark space By the
3 This Stran-ger will search for His home in the night And then

night when there's no one ex-pec-ting to see Him at all.
light of our liv-ing on earth we'll dis-cov-er His face.
how will He find it un-less all the win-dows are bright?

Keep oil in the lamps so they're rea-dy to burn On the
The face of the Mas-ter is al-ways at hand In the
But if we the wai-ting why then He'll come in And there'll

night of His sec-ret when those who are wait-ing He'll call.
face of the stran-ger, the poor, in the face of a man.
be a home-com-ing with danc-ing and sing-ing with-in.

136. When I Needed a Neighbor

Sydney Carter

Sydney Carter

1 When I need-ed a neigh-bor were you there, were you there? When I need-ed a neigh-bor were you there, were you there? And the creed and the col-or and the name won't mat-ter, Were you there?

2 I was hun-gry and thirst-y, were you there, were you there? I was hun-gry and thirst-y, were you there, were you there?

3 I was cold, I was na-ked, were you there, were you there? I was cold, I was na-ked, were you there, were you there?

4 When I need-ed a shel-ter were you there, were you there? When I need-ed a shel-ter were you there, were you there?

5 When I needed a healer were you there, were you there?

6 Wherever you travel I'll be there, I'll be there,
Wherever you travel I'll be there,
And the creed and the color and the name won't matter,
I'll be there.

To the tune of WHEN I NEEDED A NEIGHBOR

1 When they shouted hosanna, were you there, were you there?
When they shouted hosanna, were you there?

And the creed and the color and the name won't matter,
Were you there?

2 When they took me to prison, were you there, were you there?
When they took me to prison, were you there?

3 When the crosses were crooked, were you there, were you there?
When the crosses were crooked, were you there?

4 When the crosses were burning, were you there, were you there?
When the crosses were burning, were you there?

5 When I needed a neighbor, were you there, were you there?
When I needed a neighbor, were you there?

137. King of Glory, King of Peace

George Herbert (1593-1632)   Jim Minchin

1 King of glo - ry, King of peace,—
2 Where - fore with my ut - most art
3 Sev'n whole days not one in sev - en

From *Jazz in the Church, Volume 3.* Copyright © 1968 by James Minchin. Distributed by
the Presbyterian Bookroom, Melbourne, Australia.

Chords: Bb/G Gm/Em C/A Bb/G C/A

me.
me.
Thee:

Thou didst note my work-ing breast,——
And a-lone, when they re-plied,——
E'en e-ter-ni-ty's too short,——

Chords: Gm/Em C7/A7 F/D Gm7/Em7 F/D

Stanzas 1 and 2 | Stanza 3

Thou hast spared—— me.
Thou didst hear—— me.
To ex-tol—— Thee.

138. Jesus in the Morning

Traditional

Chords: G C G

1 Je-sus, Je-sus, Je-sus in the morn-ing, Je-sus at the noon-time,

Chords: G B7 Em Am7 D D7 G

Je-sus, Je-sus, Je-sus when the sun goes down.

2 Love Him   3 Serve Him   4 Thank Him   5 Praise Him

139. When Stephen, Full of Power and Grace

SALVATION

Jan Struther (1901-1953)

From Ananias Davisson's *Kentucky Harmony* (ca. 1812)

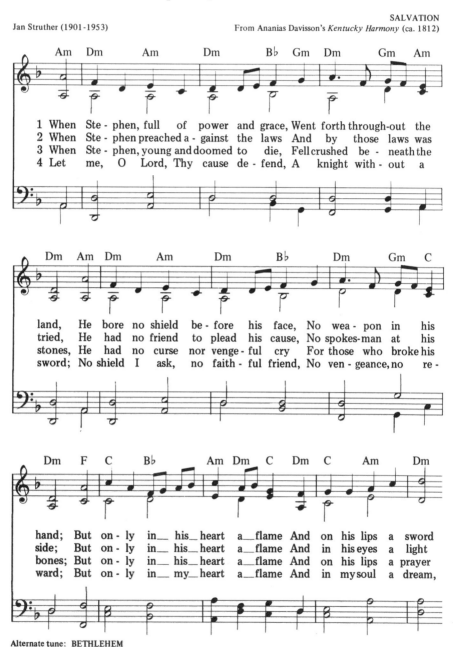

1 When Ste - phen, full of power and grace, Went forth through-out the
2 When Ste - phen preached a - gainst the laws And by those laws was
3 When Ste - phen, young and doomed to die, Fell crushed be - neath the
4 Let me, O Lord, Thy cause de - fend, A knight with - out a

land, He bore no shield be - fore his face, No wea - pon in his
tried, He had no friend to plead his cause, No spokes-man at his
stones, He had no curse nor venge - ful cry For those who broke his
sword; No shield I ask, no faith - ful friend, No ven - geance, no re -

hand; But on - ly in__ his__ heart a__flame And on his lips a sword
side; But on - ly in__ his__ heart a__flame And in his eyes a light
bones; But on - ly in__ his__ heart a__flame And on his lips a prayer
ward; But on - ly in__ my__ heart a__flame And in my soul a dream,

Alternate tune: BETHLEHEM

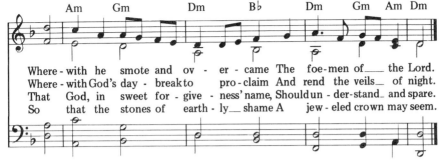

Where - with he smote and ov - er - came The foe-men of___ the Lord.
Where - with God's day - break to pro - claim And rend the veils__ of night.
That God, in sweet for - give - ness' name, Should un - der-stand_ and spare.
So that the stones of earth - ly__ shame A jew - eled crown may seem.

140. Morning Has Broken

Old Gaelic melody
Arr. by O. S.

Eleanor Farjeon (1881 –)

1 Morn - ing has bro - ken Like the first morn - ing, Black-bird has
2 Sweet the rain's new fall Sun - lit from heav - en, Like the first
3 Mine is the sun - light! Mine is the morn - ing, Born of the

spo - ken Like the first bird. Praise for the sing - ing! Praise for the
dew - fall On the first grass. Praise for the sweet - ness Of the wet
one light E - den saw play! Praise with e - la - tion, Praise ev - 'ry

morn - ing! Praise for them, spring - ing Fresh from the Word!
gar - den, Sprung in com - plete - ness Where His feet pass.
morn - ing, God's re - cre - a - tion Of the new day!

141. Where Shall I Then Thy Spirit Shun

Christopher Smart (1722-1771)
Based on Psalm 139

WEBER
James Boeringer

Intended to be sung in unison

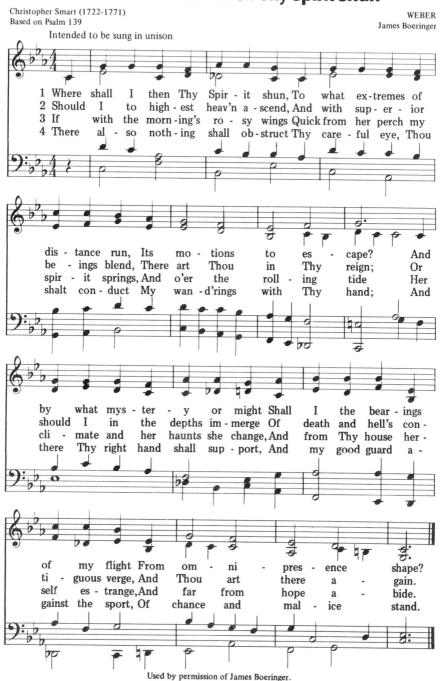

1 Where shall I then Thy Spir - it shun, To what ex-tremes of
2 Should I to high-est heav'n a - scend, And with sup - er - ior
3 If with the morn-ing's ro - sy wings Quick from her perch my
4 There al - so noth-ing shall ob-struct Thy care - ful eye, Thou

dis - tance run, Its mo - tions to es - cape? And
be - ings blend, There art Thou in Thy reign; Or
spir - it springs, And o'er the roll - ing tide Her
shalt con - duct My wan -d'rings with Thy hand; And

by what mys - ter - y or might Shall I the bear - ings
should I in the depths im - merge Of death and hell's con -
cli - mate and her haunts she change, And from Thy house her -
there Thy right hand shall sup - port, And my good guard a -

of my flight From om - ni - pres - ence shape?
ti - guous verge, And Thou art there a - gain.
self es - trange, And far from hope a - bide.
gainst the sport, Of chance and mal - ice stand.

Used by permission of James Boeringer.

5 If to the darkness I appeal,
    The darkness shall at least conceal
And quench Thy piercing ray;
    The thought convincing conscience checks,
And Thine internal truth detects,
    And turns my night to day.

6 To Thee the darkness is no gloom,
    Alike to Thee the morning's womb,
And evening's barren shade;
    Thee all created objects strike,
The dawn and the still dusk alike,
    Which their relations made.

142. Praise (It's Not God's Fault)

Edgar Schmidt

Edgar Schmidt

1 Come, all ye peo - ple, sing a hap - py song,
2 Go tell your broth - er who's in mis - er - y,
3 Go tell your sis - ter in her drudg - er - y,
4 Come, all ye peo - ple, sing a hap - py song.

Come, all ye peo - ple, shout for joy,
Go tell your broth - er not to fear.
Go tell your sis - ter not to fear.
Come, all ye peo - ple, shout for joy.

Come, all ye peo - ple, sing a hap - py
Go tell your broth - er who's in mis - er -
Go tell your sis - ter in her drudg - er -
Come, all ye peo - ple, sing a hap - py

song, The day of the Lord is near.
y, The day of the Lord is near.
y, The day of the Lord is near.
song, The day of the Lord is near.

143. Worship the Lord

Fred Kaan, 1972

Melody from Sri Lanka
Accomp., O.S.

Refrain

Wor-ship the Lord, wor-ship the Fa-ther, the Spir-it, the Son,

rais-ing our hands in de-vo-tion to Him who is One.

Stanzas

1 Rais-ing our hands as a sign of re-joic-ing,
2 Pray-ing and train-ing that we be a bless-ing,
3 Called to be part-ners with God in cre-a-tion,
4 Bring-ing the bread and the wine to the ta-ble,
5 Now in re-sponse to the life You are giv-ing,

and with our lips our to-geth-er-ness voic-ing,
and by our work-man-ship dai-ly ex-press-ing
hon-or-ing Christ as the Lord of the na-tion,
ask-ing that we may be led and en-a-bled,
help us, O Fa-ther, to of-fer our liv-ing,

giv - ing our - selves to a life of cre - a - tive - ness,
we are com - mit - ted to serv - ing hu - man - i - ty,
we must be read - y for risk and for sac - ri - fice,
tru - ly u - ni - ted, to find a new broth - er - hood,*
seek - ing a just and a heal - ing so - ci - e - ty,

wor - ship and work must be one!

*Or peoplehood

144. Rain On, Little Rain
(Little Rain)

Marji Hazen   Marji Hazen

1 Rain on, lit - tle rain, rain on, And blow, lit - tle
2 Shine down, burn - ing sun, shine down, And move, black old
3 Go down, wide riv - er, go down, And float, yel - low

wind, keep on blow - ing. Rain on, lit - tle rain;
dust, from my door. Shine on, burn - ing sun;
leaf, to the sea. Go down, wide riv - er.

Blow, lit - tle wind, The Lord on - ly knows where I'm go - ing.
Move, black old dust, The Lord on - ly knows what I'm for.
Float, yel - low leaf; The Lord on - ly knows what I'll be.

145. Ye Are Witnesses

Al Carmines

Al Carmines

And ye are wit-ness-es,— wit-ness-es of these things. And ye are wit-ness-es,— wit-ness-es of these things.— Re-pent-ance and re-mis-sion of sin

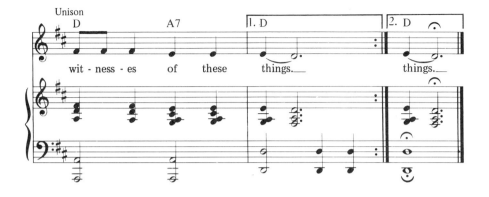

wit - ness - es   of   these   things.___   things.___

146. Sing, Sing, Praise and Sing

Elizabeth Syré

Elizabeth Syré
South Africa

Sing, sing, praise and sing! Ho - nor God for ev - 'ry - thing.

Glo - ry to the high - est King, sing and praise and sing!

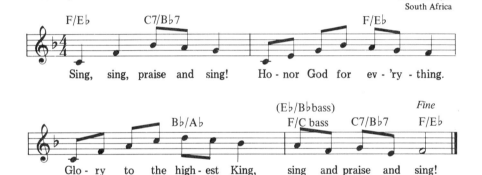

Clap	your hands,	lift	your voice,	praise	the	Lord,	and	re - joice!
Full	of	joy,	full	of	rest,	in	our	Lord,	we	are	blessed.
Are	you weak?	Ne -	ver mind!	come	and	sing,	"God	is	King!"
Love	and peace	is	so	near,	praise	the	Lord!	God	can	hear!
Cym -	bal, harp,	vi -	o - lin,	tam - bou -	rine,	all	join	in!

147. When the Church of Jesus

F. Pratt Green (1903-)

RUTH
Samuel Smith, 1865

1 When the church of Je - sus shuts its out - er door,
2 If our hearts are lift - ed, where de - vo - tion soars,
3 Lest the gifts we of - fer, mon - ey, tal - ents, time,

Lest the roar of traf - fic, drown the voice of prayer;
High a - bove this hun - gry suf - fering world of ours;
Serve to salve our con - science, to our sec - ret shame;

May our prayers, Lord, make us ten times more a - ware
Lest our hymns should drug us to for - get its needs,
Lord, re - prove, in - spire us by the way You give.

That the world we ban - ish is our Chris - tian care.
Forge our Chris - tian wor - ship in - to Chris - tian deeds.
Teach us, dy - ing Sav - ior, how true Chris - tians live.

148. Yours Is the Kingdom

Text based on the Eucharistic Prayer
of the Didache, 1st century A.D. by
J. F. M.

J. H. Miffleton
Accomp., O. S.

Refrain — *Strong beat, but not too fast* ($\quad$ = 84)

A/G   F#m/Em   A/G   F#m/Em   A/G   F#m/Em

Yours is the king-dom, Yours is the pow-er, Yours is the glo-ry

E/D   C#7/B7   D/C Bm/Am E7/D7   A/G   *Fine.*

ev - er - more!   Lord, for - ev - er,   Lord, for - ev - er - more!

Stanzas

A/G   F#m /Em   A/G   F#m/Em

Bro - ken bread is scat-tered on the hill-sides and the plains,
Blood-soaked lands are search-ing for the peace You prom-ised us,
Free - dom is Your gift for all who live and die in You,
From the ends of all the earth and out be - yond the stars,
One_____ in the bread we break and one in our con-cern,

Bm/Am   E7 /D7   Repeat refrain

Bro - ken hearts and bod - ies cry for rest._____
Or - phans of man's fol - ly cry for You._____
Free - dom is find - ing life in You._____
Gath-ered in Your pres - ence, we are one._____
One with You we cel - e - brate this day._____

Index of Sources

Topical Index

Index of First Lines and Titles